Living the Catechism of the Catholic Church

CHRISTOPH SCHÖNBORN, O.P.

Living the
Catechism of the Catholic Church

A Brief Commentary on the Catechism
for Every Week of the Year

VOLUME ONE

TRANSLATED BY DR. DAVID KIPP

IGNATIUS PRESS   SAN FRANCISCO

Title of the German original:
Herzstücke unseres Glaubens
Das "Credo" im Katechismus der Katholischen Kirche
© 1994 Wiener Dom-Verlag Gesellschaft m.b.H., Vienna

Cover by Riz Boncan Marsella

© 1995 Ignatius Press, San Francisco
ISBN 0–89870–560–6
Library of Congress catalogue number 95–75670
Printed in the United States of America

Contents

Preface

Over the course of a year, from week to week, fifty-two times, it fell to me to publish a weekly article in the Vienna Catholic newspaper on "Essential Elements of the Faith". The *Catechism of the Catholic Church* was my point of reference. That is the origin of this commentary now in the form of a book—upon Part One of the *Catechism*.

The object of the following pages is, in each short section, to bring into relief and clarify an important element of the faith. This book is offered as a help in the personal or group study of the *Catechism*. For this it is important not to lose sight of the overall context of each section.

For faith is whole. It has only one heart, one center: Jesus Christ, the Son of the living God. Christ must therefore also be the center of catechesis whose object is "putting people . . . in communion . . . with Jesus Christ: only he can lead us to the love of the Father in the Spirit and make us share in the life of the Holy Trinity" (CCC 426), for "in him are hid all the treasures of wisdom and knowledge" (Col 2:3). In a certain sense, the "essential elements of the faith" have their origin in a treasury of the heart of Jesus. This heart is the symbol of "that love with which the divine Redeemer continually loves the eternal Father and all men" without exception (CCC 478).

The brief presentations and reflections will have achieved their goal if they lead to a deeper surrender of faith, a greater love of the heart of Jesus (CCC 158, 2669).

Christoph Schönborn, O.P.

Auxiliary Bishop of Vienna

Feast of the Transfiguration of the Lord

August 6, 1994

To know God—the life of man

"Father, . . . this is eternal life, that they may know you, the only true God, and Jesus Christ whom you have sent" (Jn 17:3). These words are quoted in the epigraph to the *Catechism of the Catholic Church*, whose English edition was published in May 1994. To know God means to live. This knowing is the goal of our life. In Sacred Scripture, that goal is also expressed as "to see God" (CCC 1028).

Saint Teresa of Avila once said, as a child, "I want to see God!" And she is supposed to have added, "In order to see him, I must die" (CCC 1011). In the Old Testament, God says that "man shall not see me and live" (Ex 33:20). To see God, to know God—that means to live, but it is a living that is no longer of this world. Here on earth, in our life of pilgrimage, what John says holds true: "No one has ever seen God" (Jn 1:18). Hence, this earthly life is still not the full, true life; it is like a shadow, passing as if windblown, even when it lasts for many years.

We are, however, destined for another life, one that signifies unimaginable happiness. In his *Confessions* (which are a kind of "life confession" and a testimony, a praising of God's incomprehensible love), Saint Augustine says of this other life, "When I am completely united to you, there will be no more sorrow or trials; entirely full of you, my life will be complete" (*Confessions* 10, 28, 39; CCC 45). It is for this happiness that we were created, and this happiness is what the "restless heart"—referred to by that same Augustine—is seeking (CCC 30).

In the old catechism, the first question was: "For what purpose did God create us?"; and the answer was: "God created us to know, to love, and to serve him, and so to come to paradise" (cf. CCC 1721). This simple sentence is like a secure rope on a steep mountain pathway—something that one can hold on to when things become uncertain. I have known cases in which people who had not practiced their religion for years, even decades, were suddenly reminded, in the midst of some profound crisis in their lives, of catechism sentences like this from their childhood, words that they had then learned by heart—perhaps without much thought—and that now suddenly surfaced from memory as helpful, saving precepts.

In a quite simple manner, this first catechetical truth simultaneously illustrates the meaning of the *Catechism*: it is a pathway, a help "toward a happy life", an aid to living, a signpost, a trail map set out with precise destinations. For the early Christians, Christian life was simply "the Way" (cf. Acts 9:2; 19:9, 23; 24:14, 22)—not just one way among many, but that Way which God himself indicates to us, which leads unerringly through this life, and which allows us to arrive with certainty at our goal. In the following pages, it is this Way that will be discussed, with its beauties and joys, but also its dangers. Here, the *Catechism of the Catholic Church* will serve as a kind of map.[1]

[1] The metaphor of a map is taken from the helpful introduction to the *Catechism* by W. Krieger, *Und er bewegt uns doch* (Benno-Verlag, 1994), 96.

2

What is the Catechism?

In India, at the start of 1993, I was presented with a copy of a book that has become a best-seller there. It is entitled *Daddy, Am I a Hindu?* This question is put into the mouth of a boy who is asking his father every possible sort of question about their religion, Hinduism. The result is a kind of "catechism" for Hindus, in the familiar form of questions and answers, which has obviously aroused the interest of a great many people—I even noticed that it was being sold by a department store in the United States. Is that not a "sign of the times"? Evidently it is not only Christians who are searching today for a deeper and better knowledge of their own religion. In a world that is growing smaller, in which borders and distances are being overcome by technology and communication, many people are asking again about their own roots, about what foundations can support that house which is their life. This need not be quickly dismissed as "fundamentalism". It is a good, healthy reaction when people begin to seek anew for the foundations of their own religion and, thus, of their own lives.

Books of this kind have existed since the beginning of Christianity. It was only later that they were named "catechisms", but they served the same purpose from the first: to lay, and to reinforce, the foundations of the Christian faith. These concise, comprehensible outlines of Christian religious teaching were usually the result of rich experience in practical transmission of the faith (CCC 8). Although no book can replace that living ministry, books can be of assistance to it. Personal communion with Christ and a love of man that springs from the faith are the most convincing means of catechesis (CCC 427). Pope John Paul I, who was a gifted catechist, dedicated his book on catechesis to his mother: "In loving memory of my mother, my first catechist" (cf. CCC 25).

This is not to suggest that "catechisms" are superfluous. In order to be able to transmit the faith, we must be familiar with it, and simple, clear outlines of the doctrines of the faith are necessary for that (CCC 23). In view of the great uncertainty, as well as ignorance, that often prevails regarding religious matters, the bishops asked the Holy Father, at the Synod in 1985, whether it might not be advisable that a book on the faith be composed, a catechism for the entire Church, which would provide a reliable source of guidance, a central orientational point, for catechesis (CCC 10): the *Catechism of the Catholic Church*.

✶ What purposes can this new *Catechism* serve? The first and most important goal is surely a deepening of personal faith. We can love only that which we know, while the more we love, the more deeply we wish to know; and out of this arises a desire to communicate that which we love to others. Christ is the center of catechesis; living communion with him is the goal of all catechesis (CCC 426). This is the first aim of the *Catechism*: to know the love of Christ that surpasses all knowledge (cf. Eph 3:19). That is why the *Catechism* begins with the profession of faith, the Creed, which speaks of God the Father, his Son Jesus Christ, and the Holy Spirit. Hence, the short meditations that follow will be concerned primarily with the "heart" of our faith, with Christ. It is from him that all Christian life originates (CCC 478).

3

Seeking and finding God

It is a surprising observation: the Church teaches that we can know with certainty the existence of God (CCC 36). Our reason can lead us to the certain insight that God exists. In other words, it is not through revelation that we are first able to know God but already through our natural cognitive faculty. This doctrine gives expression to a great trust in man. The Church has time and again defended the dignity and capacity of that rational faculty which God has bestowed on man.

What a great miracle our reason is! Is it not astonishing when something suddenly becomes "clear" to us? Or when a young person whom we are teaching suddenly "sees" some relevant point? Einstein is said to have once remarked: "The amazing thing is not that we should know the world but that it should be knowable." It is amazing how a child keeps "mulling over" a thing until he succeeds in "grasping" it. An adult researcher basically does nothing different. But even more amazing is the fact that we can grasp reality, that we are able to penetrate it and run up against, not chaos, but, rather, constantly new, constantly more magnificent forms of order (CCC 283). The more deeply researchers penetrate the various sectors of reality, the more astonishingly the order of creation emerges (CCC 299).

We are able to know this order because it exists. The world is not a blind jumble, but a "cosmos", that is, an ordered, "adorned", beautiful reality (CCC 32). The amazing thing is that we no longer find this amazing! Is it just a matter of course that the immense universe should contain our "temperate planet" Earth, that this planet should possess the extremely improbable conditions that make life possible on it? And how much more amazing is it that we humans should exist, we who can know all this and wonder at it? Whoever has the capacity to be overwhelmed by such wonder can exclaim with the Psalm: "O Lord, our Lord, how majestic is thy name in all the earth!" (Ps 8:9).

The philosophers have rightly identified wonder as the origin of philosophy. Sacred Scripture goes farther, saying that fear of God is the origin of wisdom and that only "the fool says in his heart, 'There is no God' " (Ps 14:1). Saint Thomas Aquinas holds that God is actually the "most knowable" reality, since nothing has more radiance, clarity, and truth than God himself. Therefore, no knowledge satisfies our longing so abundantly as does knowledge of God (CCC 1718). Seeing and knowing him will be our perfect happiness: heaven (CCC 1024).

But why, then, is our knowledge of God often so faint and cloudy as to make God seem an unreal idea? The causes of this are many. Our reason is weak, we remain preoccupied with what is immediately before us, we cling to the sensory surface of things. Above all, however, we are crippled by an intellectual lethargy, stemming from original sin, that allows us to shirk the efforts and sacrifices involved in seeking the truth (CCC 37). In order to know God, we must seek him, which requires a willing with all our power. But that is lacking in us. God has certainly given us the reason and will with which to seek and find him. Yet we would remain, for our part, "in darkness and in the shadow of death" (Lk 1:79) had he not accommodated himself to us in a wholly new way: through his revelation.

4

God reveals himself

Every man can seek God and also find him, "he is not far from each one of us, for 'In him we live and move and have our being'" (as the Apostle Paul says to the Athenians, Acts 17:28). Yet this seeking remains a groping that often goes astray and thus leads to false gods. Therefore God has chosen another way: he himself seeks man, seeks him like the shepherd in the parable of the lost sheep. He himself approaches man and makes himself known—he reveals himself to him (CCC 50).

The Christian faith rests on revelation. "What no eye has seen, nor ear heard, nor the heart of man conceived" (1 Cor 2:9) has been revealed by God. Revelation—that means first of all that God makes himself known and thereby communicates himself. These two aspects belong inseparably together: that God proclaims something of himself that we could not have known by our own powers, and that he thereby simultaneously presents himself to us (CCC 142). When we will come to know and see God as he is, then we will also—in an inexpressibly blissful way—be wholly in communion with him. Then God will be wholly "revealed" to us.

God has revealed himself gradually, by stages (CCC 53). Although he gives all men evidence of himself in the things of creation, the history of God's revelation as such begins with the calling of Abraham. With that one man, the father of all the faithful, God makes a covenant. Abraham will be the ancestral father of the people of Israel, whom God makes the trustees of the promise (CCC 59). God chooses one out of many, one people out of the many peoples, to be presented with the revelation of his will. To this one, chosen people falls the task of being, in the midst of all humanity, the bearer of revelation. Through this one people, all peoples are to be blessed and to arrive at the knowledge of God (CCC 62).

Among the people of Israel, God made another special choice. Out of all the Israelites, he selected one individual in order to reveal to her his eternal decision, "the mystery of his will", namely, the Virgin Mary (CCC 488). Through her and with her consent, he would complete his revelation—through Jesus Christ.

What revelation means becomes really understandable to us only through Christ. He is God's Son, his eternal Word. In that Word, God tells us everything he wants to tell us; even more, he declares himself, as it were, totally. Christ is the "fullness of all revelation" (CCC 65). It consists not solely of words, it is a Person: Jesus Christ. In him, God has not just communicated something about himself and his mystery but has bestowed himself wholly.

This is why the Council states that revelation has been completed with Christ and that "no new public revelation is to be expected before the glorious manifestation of our Lord Jesus Christ" (CCC 66). We will never have exhausted the richness of Christ, he will never be surpassed. Hence, so-called "private" revelations (CCC 67), assuming that they are genuine, never yield anything new that was not already contained in the revelation of Christ. They can, however, contribute to quickening our faith in Christ, to rekindling our love of him (as in the case of the Heart of Jesus revelations to Saint Margaret Mary Alacoque).

5

Sacred Scripture

One sometimes hears the comment that Christianity is a "religion of the book", like Judaism and Islam, that is, that all three religions share the element of being based on a sacred book inspired ("inspirited") by God: the Bible of the Old Testament for Judaism, that of the Old and New Testaments for Christianity, and the Koran for Islam.

This characterization of Christianity is, however, not strictly accurate. The Christian faith is not directed toward a book; it is not based on any written words but on the living Word of God. The center of our faith is the Person of the eternal Word, of the Son of God, who became a man for our sake (CCC 108). In him God has told us everything and given us everything. Jesus Christ is our living book, he is God's Word for men (CCC 102).

Yet God at first revealed this Word only gradually. He wanted to make allowances for our weakness. Thus he bent down to us like a father to his children. He adapted his Word to our powers of understanding. In the Old Testament, he spoke to his people through selected men of God; and much of what God had done for his people, and said to them through his prophets, was gradually recorded in various books, which make up the Old Testament today (CCC 122).

Ultimately, however, God spoke to all men through his own Son. That is why the words and deeds of Jesus are so important to us. In them, God's eternal Word comes to expression in human words. What Jesus did and said has been reliably and faithfully handed down by his disciples; for they wanted to lead many people to Jesus Christ, their beloved master, who had gathered them around him and shared his life with them. At first, it was surely by word of mouth that the disciples passed on what they knew of Jesus and what he had taught them. But they soon began to record much of this in writing as well. Thus the Gospels gradually came into being (CCC 126).

When we consider this, it is quite evident that the apostles and their colleagues are communicating historically reliable things about Jesus in the Gospels. The clear image of the Lord as they had known him loomed too large before their eyes, the impression left by his words and his gestures, indeed, by his entire figure, was too powerful, for them to have even thought of adapting their image of him in any way to what would correspond with the "spirit of the times". Therefore, at the Second Vatican Council, the Church "unhesitatingly affirms" the "historicity" of the Gospels (*Dei Verbum* no. 19).

Still, the reliability of Sacred Scripture rests, not solely on the credibility of the witnesses, but also on the work of the Holy Spirit. As the Council teaches: The Church, "relying on the faith of the apostolic age, accepts as sacred and canonical the books of the Old and the New Testaments, whole and entire, with all their parts, on the grounds that, written under the inspiration of the Holy Spirit, they have God as their author and have been handed on as such to the Church herself" (CCC 105). Sacred Scripture is formally celebrated in the liturgy as the Word of the living God (CCC 103). It is God's Word expressed in the words of men (CCC 101).

6

Interpretation of Sacred Scripture

"In Sacred Scripture, God speaks to man in a human way. To interpret Scripture correctly, the reader must be attentive to what the human authors truly wanted to affirm and to what God wanted to reveal to us by their words"—thus we read in the *Catechism* (CCC 109).

The Council cites a leading principle for all interpretation of Scripture: "Sacred Scripture must be read and interpreted in the light of the same Spirit by whom it was written" (CCC 111). In order to understand Scripture correctly, it must be read as inspired by the Holy Spirit. It is meant to be read in faith, just as it also arose from faith and testifies to faith.

This requires first of all precise attention to what has been called the "literal sense" of Sacred Scripture: to that which the authors of the biblical texts intended to express. Saint Thérèse of Lisieux wished that she had learned Greek and Hebrew in order to be able to understand exactly what Sacred Scripture states. It is also helpful to compare different translations of Scripture in order to gain a closer feeling for the intended sense of the words. A good knowledge of the history of the times—especially that of the Jewish people, their environment, their customs, their social conditions—will contribute much to one's understanding.

Attentiveness to differences of so-called "literary genre" is also helpful: Is there, for example, a parable involved, a historical narrative, a prophetic oration? In just which form of expression has the author clothed his statement? In what sort of situation has he written? To whom, in particular, is he addressing himself? Inquiry into all this is important for grasping just what the authors of Sacred Scripture wanted to express and have actually given expression to (CCC 110).

Scholarly exegesis plays an irreplaceable role in facilitating correct understanding of Scripture. How often we find that, as a result of more precise insight into historical and linguistic meanings, a scriptural passage begins to acquire new light and the religious statement emerges more clearly. Yet purely historical or linguistic analysis is not sufficient. Scholarship and faith must go hand in hand if the religious testimony of Scripture is to be grasped.

For this, the Council indicates three criteria:

1. Be especially attentive "to the content and unity of the whole Scripture". Scripture is one totality. All its parts are bound up with one another. One must not, for instance, isolate one Gospel, or even one passage, from the totality (CCC 112).

2. Read the Scripture within "the living tradition of the whole Church". We are not the first to read the Bible. How have the great masters interpreted it: an Augustine, a Thomas Aquinas, a Newman? How has

Scripture been understood in the course of the Church's long religious experience (CCC 113)?

3. Be attentive to the analogy of faith; that is, to those aids to understanding that the faith confers on us. The lives of the saints provide the most concretely vivid interpretation of Scripture (CCC 114). Francis is a living commentary on the Gospels. The miracles of the Gospels have thousands of echoes in the miracles of the saints. Whoever reflects, for example, on the life of Saint Bernadette of Lourdes learns to read the gospel in the same spirit in which it was written.

7

Faith—the response of man

God first loved us. Before we were, he had chosen us to be and to live, to know and to love him. Before we knew him, he had made himself known to us. Before we could respond to him, he had called us. He makes his approach to us. To respond to him is faith (CCC 142).

Faith has something to do with obedience, with both listening and relating to the God who addresses us. Abraham is the prototype of this sort of believing obedience (CCC 145). God calls to him, and he obeys. That is faith, and the great thing about this attitude is the unconditional trust in the one whom he faithfully obeys. Like Abraham, and even more than he, Mary believed God. She had complete trust that nothing is impossible for God. She gave herself over completely to his will: "Let it be [done] to me according to your word" (CCC 148).

To have faith in God with all one's heart, with all one's intellect and will (CCC 143), means to honor God, to glorify him. Whoever believes God also acknowledges God's greatness, omnipotence, and love, and submits himself to God. When Jesus encounters

27

men who believe him wholly and utterly, he is filled with wonder. A really believing man is great because he believes God capable of every great thing.

Man can undertake such a fully trusting submission of his own life only in relation to God (CCC 150). It would be demanding too much of one's neighbor, even if he were the dearest of persons, to want to expect everything of him in the way that we may expect everything, in faith, of God. That holds true even regarding the Church. As the *Catechism* says: "In the Apostles' Creed we profess 'one Holy Church' (*Credo . . . Ecclesiam*), and not to believe *in* the Church, so as not to confuse God with his works and to attribute clearly to God's goodness *all* the gifts he has bestowed on his Church" (CCC 750).

We believe in no one but God: the Father, the Son, and the Holy Spirit (CCC 178). By trusting God in this way, however, we also assent, in faith, to what he has revealed and bestowed. Being able to believe is itself such a gift. We say that faith is a grace (CCC 153). As a result of this unearned gift, however, we also bear a responsibility. It is a talent that we must somehow put to use. Our faith ought to grow, and mature, and produce fruit. It can decay if our lives are not actually lived from within it. It can wither if it is not constantly invigorated through prayer. It can gain strength through trials, grow deep-rooted through the patient and persistent doing of good; through love it ripens, through hope it becomes steadfast, even in times of darkness and affliction (CCC 162).

Faith is more than an experience. There are often periods in which we sense and undergo little, in which our feelings remain barren. This need not be a hindrance to faith but can instead clarify it. I believe, not because I have feelings, but because I accord belief to God himself, who is believable beyond all measure (CCC 156). The saints have often lived through that "dark night" in which all experiences vanished and only faith remained (CCC 164). Precisely then does that unconditional love of God become manifest which perseveres faithfully in belief even through periods of aridity and darkness. God will not withhold his reward for such faithfulness: he himself will be that reward (CCC 2011).

8

". . . Look upon the faith of your Church"

After the Our Father, we pray in the liturgy of the
Holy Mass: "Look not upon our sins, but upon the
faith of your Church." That formulation can be surprising. "Faith of the Church"—by this we usually understand the doctrinal structure, the entirety of that which
the Church teaches. Here, however, something different is meant: the Church herself is understood as a believer, in a way as a believing person, as distinct from
"our sins", from us sinners. Who is this Church, upon
whose faith the Lord is entreated to look?

We can pose this question in another form: When
we make our profession of faith at Holy Mass, we all
say simultaneously, "I believe. . . ." Here, each one
speaks for himself personally, since believing is a quite
personal act. Nevertheless, what we express in the
Creed is not our "private" ideas but something shared
by us all in the faith. We could also say, "We believe
. . .", as is done in the Greek version of the "major"
profession of faith. And yet, this "We" is not simply the
sum of all our personal conceptions of belief—in the
way, for example, that a political party reaches consen-
sus on some platform and then calls it "our" platform.

"We believe" what the Church believes, that which she has received from her Lord and Master, Jesus Christ, and to which she faithfully and lovingly adheres.

Hence, the expression "I believe . . ." refers in the first instance to the "I" of the Church. I, as an individual, can join in saying the "I believe . . ." only within the communion of the Church. My belief is supported by the belief of the many who have believed before me and have handed on the faith. I have not given myself faith, just as I have also not given myself life (CCC 166). And just as I have not made my life myself but have received it, so neither can I invent my faith myself but can only accept it. I have received it from the Church, just as I have received my life from my mother. During baptism, the question is put: "What do you ask of God's Church?" And the answer is: "Faith." "What does faith offer you?" "Eternal life" (CCC 168).

There would be no common faith if there were no common language of faith. While we do not believe in formulas, we nevertheless express what we believe in words and sentences that we share in common and that make it possible for us to speak of what we believe. It is, therefore, indispensable to have a binding, common language of faith, just as the bond of language is necessary to human society (CCC 170).

What would our liturgy be without the treasure of a common religious language? And how could the faith be proclaimed and transmitted if each of us were to engage in his own "linguistic games"? The religious language is also the living remembrance of religious realities. In its essentials, it reaches back to Christ, who spoke to us in his own words of God's Kingdom (CCC 543). The Church preserves the memory of this. "As a mother who teaches her children to speak and so to understand and communicate, the Church our Mother teaches us the language of faith in order to introduce us to the understanding and the life of faith" (CCC 171).

9

I believe in God

It is with the above words that the profession of faith begins. They are fundamental to all that follows them and contain in a certain way the entire Creed (CCC 199). Everything that is specifically cited in the Creed depends on belief in God. Thus the Letter to the Hebrews states: "Without faith it is impossible to please him [God]. For whoever would draw near to God must believe that he exists and that he rewards those who seek him" (Heb 11:6).

Rudolf Bultmann—the great, if also controversial, Protestant exegete—coined the phrase that God is "the all-determining reality". If God exists, then he alone can be our "one and all", then all that we are and all that we possess must come from, and be in, his hand. Conversely, what Ivan Karamazov says in Dostoyevsky's novel would hold true: "If God does not exist, then everything is permitted"; and, as we can add here, "everything is meaningless".

As a child, Saint Thomas Aquinas is supposed to have asked the question, "Who is God?" Throughout his life that question never ceased to occupy him. When, as a theologian, he speaks of God, one can always sense, behind all the sobriety of his words, a deep reverence for God. In Sacred Scripture, such reverence is called "fear of God", and it is seen as "the beginning of wisdom". Reverence before the greatness and holiness of God has always overcome men when, with searching and open hearts, they have come up against the mystery of God.

Thus Moses takes off his sandals and veils his face as he becomes aware of the presence of God in the burning bush. Isaiah behaves similarly when God calls him to be a prophet. Before the greatness of God's magnificence, which he is allowed to look upon, he cries out: "Woe is me! I am lost; for I am a man of unclean lips" (Is 6:5). And it is the same for Peter when he experiences the miraculous catch of fish: "Depart from me, for I am a sinful man, O Lord" (Lk 5:8). In the presence of the holy, man becomes frightened and senses his own insignificance (CCC 208).

And yet, in the encounter with the presence of God, things do not remain at the stage of this "holy terror". In the burning bush, God reveals himself to Moses as "I AM WHO I AM" (Ex 3:14). He promises him: "I will be with you" (Ex 3:12). He reveals himself as "a merciful and gracious" God, "abounding in steadfast love and faithfulness" (Ex 34:6). God's greatness and nearness, his holiness and his mercifulness, belong together (CCC 210).

Everything earthly alters, is caught up in a ceaseless coming and going. Similarly inconstant is our heart, as we often learn through painful experience. This makes it all the more consoling to know, in faith, that God persists. The psalmist prays: "They [heaven and earth] will perish, but thou dost endure" (Ps 102:26). "God is 'He who Is', from everlasting to everlasting, and as such remains ever faithful to himself and to his promises" (CCC 212). He cannot deceive, for he is truth itself; he cannot disappoint us, for he is love.

Saint Teresa of Avila gave wonderful expression to this in her well-known "bookmark", which is cited in the *Catechism* (227):

> Let nothing trouble you
> Let nothing frighten you,
> Everything passes,
> God never changes.
> Patience
> Obtains all.
> Whoever has God
> Wants for nothing.
> God alone is enough.

Jesus established his
Church as his authority
on Earth. Peter the
Head of the Church -
teaching Body of Church is
the Magisterium - handed
down Pope Bishops priests. Deacons
from the apostle

God is triune

Christians confess that "Jesus Christ is Lord" (Phil 2:11). We believe that Jesus is "the Son of the living God" (Mt 16:16). We worship him as "My Lord and my God" (Jn 20:28). And yet we say "I believe in one God".

More and more often, Christians are confronted with the question of how belief in one God can be reconciled with believing that Jesus is God's eternal Son, that he is himself God, and that the Holy Spirit is also worshipped and glorified along with the Father and the Son, and is also God. For Islam, this is a contradiction, even worse, a heresy. God is *one*: that prohibits worshipping Jesus as the Son of God and as God. For Judaism, too, this is unacceptable.

We are baptized and begin our prayer "in the name of the Father and of the Son and of the Holy Spirit"; not "in the names" (plural), but "in the name" (singular). For we do not believe in three Gods but, rather, that God is triune: Father, Son, and Holy Spirit (CCC 233).

To believe in the Most Holy Trinity is not possible by the mere means of reason; this mystery transcends reason wholly and utterly. And yet, when we accept it in faith, we discover it to be the all-illumining light: "O blessed light, O Trinity and first Unity!"—thus the Church prays in a hymn for Evening Prayer (CCC 257). God's innermost mystery is that he is the Trinity, and everything that we believe about God and his works is interfused with this mystery.

"The grace of the Lord Jesus Christ and the love of God and the fellowship of the Holy Spirit be with you all" (2 Cor 13:14). We are familiar with the Apostle's greeting here from the liturgy of the Holy Mass. "The love of God" the Father is the first origin of everything. God is love, and everything springs from his unending love, above all his eternal Son and the Holy Spirit. In himself, God is the mystery of fruitful love. The Son is eternally begotten of the Father, not as a creature, but as "light from light, true God from true God" (CCC 242). The Spirit proceeds eternally from both, the third Divine Person, "one and equal" with the Father and the Son (CCC 245).

Because of this unity of being, the Father is entirely in the Son and entirely in the Holy Spirit, and vice versa. They are really the one God. Hence, everything that God effects is the work of the Trinity. The Father never acts apart from the Son and the Holy Spirit, yet each Divine Person acts in his own proper way: "one God and Father *from* whom all things are, and one Lord Jesus Christ *through* whom all things are, and one Holy Spirit *in* whom all things are" (CCC 258). From the Father's love everything originates; through the Son we receive all the Father's grace and love (cf. Jn 1:14, 18); and just as Father and Son are one in the communion of the Holy Spirit, so all who are touched by Christ's grace are included in this communion (CCC 1997).

The first and last goal of all God's work is that we should come to know and love God and thus, now and forevermore, gain entry into the blessed communion of the one and triune God (CCC 260).

11

God our Father

"I believe in God the Father . . ."—these are the words with which the Apostles' Creed begins. That we may address God as "Father" is the "heart" of Jesus' revelation. He himself says "Father" to God in so personal and distinctive a way that the early Church retained the Aramaic original of the word in its prayers: "Abba" (Rom 8:15; Gal 4:6). She did so because Jesus prayed to, and spoke of, God in that way, and because he himself had taught his disciples to address God as "our Father".

What does this form of prayer address mean? Is it just one image among others? Is it exchangeable, in the sense that we could just as well address God as "our Mother"? That this is so is occasionally maintained today, but such a claim does not hold up.

The precise sense in which God is "Father" was revealed to us by Jesus. Through that term, Jesus not only expresses his own innermost relationship with God but also reveals the kind of relationship with God to which we are called. "Abba" is a children's word, like our "daddy". It is an expression of intimate familiarity. At the same time, however, it has connotations of great reverence. We see this in Jesus' prayer at Gethsemani (CCC 612): "Abba, Father, all things are possible to thee; remove this cup from me; yet not what I will, but what thou wilt" (Mk 14:36). All the way up to Jesus' last words of prayer, God remains for him the "Father": "Father, forgive them; for they know not what they do" (Lk 23:34); "Father, into thy hands I commit my spirit" (Lk 23:46). The words of the twelve-year-old Jesus in the temple (CCC 534) are already suggestive of a life being lived from within a relationship to the "Father" that determines everything else: "Did you not know that I must be in my Father's house?" (Lk 2:49).

Jesus himself identified the foundation of this relationship: "No one knows the Son except the Father, and no one knows the Father except the Son and anyone to whom the Son chooses to reveal him" (Mt 11:27). That means, however, that no man, no creature, has ever had a relationship to God of comparable intimacy (CCC 240). Jesus is "God's Son" and God is Jesus' Father in a unique way: "I and the Father are one" (Jn 10:30).

Hence, Jesus' use of the address "Father" expresses something that points infinitely beyond any earthly parenthood. God is, from all eternity, the Father of the only begotten Son, who is "consubstantial with the Father" and thus "true God from true God" (CCC 242). When Jesus speaks of his Father, he is not a mere man speaking of God but the eternal, incarnated Son of God speaking of his eternal Father, with whom, in the Holy Spirit, he is one God.

Regarding his loving relationship with his creatures, God can be represented through fatherly as well as motherly attributes (CCC 239). If Jesus teaches us to worship *his Father* as also *our Father*, then this form of address cannot be exchanged for any other, for it connotes something miraculous beyond all human comprehension: through the Holy Spirit we receive, as Paul says, "the spirit of sonship" (Rom 8:15). This signifies not a sense of sexual qualification (as male), but, rather, our being granted participation in the eternal relationship of the Son to the Father (CCC 2780): through Jesus, we are taken up into the innermost, blessed life of the triune God.

12

God is almighty

In the Apostles' Creed, only one attribute of God the Father is mentioned: he is "almighty". Why are no other attributes of God mentioned, for instance, his goodness, his mercifulness, and above all his love, which is so strongly characteristic of God that Saint John says: "God is love" (1 Jn 4:8)? Why should the Creed mention precisely God's omnipotence, which often carries "negative overtones" today?

The *Catechism* devotes a brief section—but one that is very important for the whole of belief—to this attribute of God (268–78). For believing that God is really almighty is a matter of great significance to our lives. One must even say that if we do not believe that God is almighty, then we do not at all believe in God's existence.

The worshippers in the Old Testament were filled with the conviction that God is truly almighty: "He does whatever he pleases" (Ps 115:3). God is "strong and mighty" (Ps 24:8). A profound sense of God's greatness is expressed in the Psalms. The prayer of the Church is filled with the same spirit. It often begins with the words: "Almighty, eternal God . . . ."

The term "almighty" reminds many of despotism, blind power, oppressive mastery. In biblical and ecclesial prayers, it has quite a different ring. Precisely because God is almighty and eternal, worshippers can turn to him with utter trust. In whom should one take refuge if not in him who "can do all things" (Job 42:2)? This might contains no trace of arbitrariness and caprice. God's omnipotence cannot be separated from his goodness, his righteousness, and his mercifulness. In the Creed, we call God the "almighty Father". Amid the tribulations of this world, it is a source of consolation and reassurance to look up to him.

To be sure, the experience of misfortune, suffering, and evil can shake one's faith in the goodness of God's omnipotence. Why does God not prevent the many sufferings on this earth, since he is, after all, the Almighty? Man's wisdom falls silent before this question. God himself, however, has answered it—through Jesus Christ. The greatest miracle of his omnipotence was performed when he sent his Son into the impotence and poverty of the Incarnation and the Cross. "Lord, you reveal your mighty power most of all by your forgiveness and compassion"—these words are from one of the Church's Collects. There is no greater demonstration of God's omnipotence than his love, out of which Christ has offered up his life for us.

Believing in the omnipotence of God is the basis for everything else that we profess in the Creed. How are we to believe that God created heaven and earth if he is not almighty? And how believe in the work of Christ—

that he became man, died for us, and really rose again? And how believe that the Holy Spirit can transform us through his grace, if we do not, with Mary, affirm in faith the message of the angel: "For with God nothing will be impossible" (Lk 1:37)?

13

God the Creator

"In the beginning God created the heavens and the earth" (Gen 1:1). Who is not moved by these powerful words with which Sacred Scripture opens? The first of all God's works is creation. It is, in a way, the model and basis for all of God's further acts. Apart from it, redemption and salvation would have no foundation (CCC 279).

The long readings for the Easter Vigil always begin with the account of creation. This world, which God has created, he has, through the death and Resurrection of Jesus his Son, also redeemed. Like the liturgy, catechesis and preaching have, for centuries, begun with the belief in God, the Creator of heaven and earth. We are discovering this anew today. Without belief in God the Creator, belief in Jesus Christ is "groundless". That is why catechesis on creation is of major importance.

To the question of why God created the world, the *Catechism* answers: "The world was created for the glory of God" (CCC 293). How often we extol the magnificence of God in his creation: "The heavens are telling the glory of God . . . " (Ps 19:1). Not because God might have need of our praise in order to increase his glory, but out of pure benevolence, in order to communicate the magnificence of his eternal beatitude, he created everything from nothing. The world is not a by-product of mere chance, but the expression of freely self-giving wisdom and love.

"O Lord, how manifold are thy works! In wisdom hast thou made them all" (Ps 104:24). What the worshipper in this psalm acknowledges is, in fact, constantly presupposed by us. We proceed on the assumption that the world is ordered according to laws that we can attempt to discover. Our whole natural-scientific conception of the universe is built upon this assumption. Accident cannot be scientifically researched, but order can; and the latter is the expression of an ordering intelligence. Creation bespeaks the wisdom of the Creator (CCC 295).

We can become receptive to the language of creation, although not apart from a purification of our outlook and heart. It is no accident that the saints have a quite special relationship with creation: Saint Francis is the best-known example. When we are under the spell of ourselves, obsessed by desire and covetousness, then creation cannot disclose itself to us in all its purity. Only he who is freed from himself begins to perceive created things properly (CCC 299). The Creator starts to speak to him in the language of his creatures, and praise of the Creator wells up in his heart.

Is it not strange that one of the most beautiful songs of praise to creation should come from someone who was suffering and close to death? When Francis prayed the *Canticle of the Creatures* (CCC 344) in San Damiano, he was racked by pain and almost blind. Suffering and adversity had purified him to the extent that he could perceive the language of God's love in the whole of creation. That is not romanticism but praise of creation despite, and transcendent beyond, suffering. But why has the good Creator allowed corruption and evil to find their way into his work?

14

God's providence

"If God the Father almighty, the Creator of the ordered and good world, cares for all his creatures, why does evil exist?" (CCC 309). "But why did God not create a world so perfect that no evil could exist in it?" (CCC 310).

No one escapes the question of why evil exists. And no answer will be able, here on earth, to resolve all such enigmas. We will understand wholly only when we see God; here and now, our comprehension remains piecemeal. And yet we are not simply abandoned, without answer, to contend with the darkness of evil. The witness of the saints is clear and luminous: all attest that nothing happens to us except through God's providence. Their lives all manifest what they also teach, namely, a great, boundless trust in the power and goodness of God's providence. They take the Sermon on the Mount at face value: "Therefore do not be anxious, saying 'What shall we eat?' or 'What shall we drink?' . . . Your heavenly Father knows that you need them all" (Mt 6:31–32).

The attitude of surrender to the will of the heavenly Father is a central element of Jesus' preaching. That is why he also taught us to pray: "Thy will be done on earth as it is in heaven" (CCC 2822). He has promised to give us "everything else as well" if only we seek his Kingdom first and above all (cf. Mt 6:33).

What is the "providence" in which we are to trust? That this term was misused during the Nazi period in Germany should not prevent us from using it properly. We call "providence" those dispositions by which God guides his creation toward perfection (CCC 302). For God would not be the Creator were he simply to abandon his work to its destiny—like an architect who hands over a house when it is ready to be occupied and then has nothing more to do with it. God is the Creator not only inasmuch as he determines the beginning of all things, calls them into being out of nothing, but also inasmuch as he sustains them in being and guides them to their final end. All creatures, even those who turn away from God, remain entirely in his hand (CCC 301).

God's providence is concretely immediate: even the least of things count in it, such as the sparrows—and our hairs (Mt 10:29–30). All our powers, too, and even our will are in God's hand (CCC 303). He grants to his creatures their capacity to act effectively; it is his providential intent that we should use what he has given us for our own benefit. We are permitted to participate in his providence. We do this through every one of our good works (CCC 306; 1951).

Mysteriously, however, even our evil actions do not fall outside of God's providence. In ways that he alone knows, he permits evil and yet turns it, in the end, to good (cf. Gen 45:8; 50:20). This mystery reaches its peak in the greatest evil that was ever done: the murder of God's own Son on the Cross (CCC 312). God has turned this deed to good, in fact, to the best: "We adore thee, O Christ, and we bless thee, because by thy Holy Cross thou hast redeemed the world."

15

The angels

"Stay, you angels, stay with me"—thus begins a moving aria from Bach's cantata for the feast of the Archangel Michael. Walter Nigg writes as follows on this: "Bach obviously sensed that something quite central was in danger of becoming lost to Christianity. It seemed to him that the angels would gradually take leave of man. He felt this to be a serious calamity. . . . What are we ever to do if the angels do not stay with us, if we are left alone without their care and help?"

Are the angels among those things that constitute the "central elements of the faith"? They are certainly not the center of our faith. Nor are we! The center of the faith is the mystery of the threefold God and the mystery of Jesus Christ, true God and true man. Everything else revolves around this center, including the angels. And ourselves! No angel will dispute this (except the "fallen angels", who have fallen because they made themselves the center—but more about that later); on the contrary, the splendor and joy of the angels consist in the very fact that their lives are directed wholly toward this center, that they serve the living God and worship the mystery of Christ with their whole being.

Hence, angels are real, and their existence is a truth of faith (CCC 328). And just as the heart does not exist for itself alone, neither does the center of the faith. The existence of angels is a certainty of the faith, a part of its living organism; and, like all the truths of faith, knowledge of the purely spiritual creatures of God is also a help to us in our lives. This is attested to, above all, by the whole of Sacred Scripture.

The history of salvation is unthinkable apart from the angels. To us, their nature is mysterious and incomprehensible because they are purely spiritual beings. They have a special closeness to God, which is why, in the Old Testament, God often appears, and speaks, through his angels. When we consider the many appearances of angels in the Bible (cf. CCC 332–33), we should be careful not to assume too quickly that they are "only" expressions of the worldview of those times. Rather, we should ask ourselves whether our religious sensitivity to the reality of angels might not have been dulled in comparison to that of earlier believers.

The life of Jesus is surrounded by the service of angels, from the Annunciation and his birth to the agony at Gethsemani, Easter morning, and the Ascension. The same applies to the life of the Church and the Christian. "Beside each believer stands an angel as protector and shepherd leading him to life", Saint Basil says, thereby affirming belief in the "guardian angel" that God has provided to accompany every man (CCC 336). "Give heed to him and hearken to his voice, do not rebel against him", God says to his people and thus to each of us (Ex 23:21). Just as (in the "*Sanctus*") we join our voices to theirs in praise, so our path through life should, in unity with them, lead surely to its goal. Thus the Church also prays that the angels might continue to accompany us beyond death and all the way to paradise (CCC 1020).

16

Heaven and earth

In the Creed, we profess that God has created "heaven and earth". This expression stands for creation "in its entirety", or, as the Nicene Creed makes explicit, "all that is, seen and unseen". One part of unseen creation has already been discussed here, namely, the angels, the purely spiritual creatures. Still to be discussed is man, who combines the seen and the unseen orders of the world in himself.

The visible world, in turn, includes "heaven and earth", the cosmos beyond us, the firmament, and the world in which we live, the planet Earth. The faith tells us that all this has been created (CCC 326). Just *how* heaven and earth, how the universe, came into being—about this there are numerous scientific findings, hypotheses, and theories. Did the universe begin with a "big bang"? Is it still continuing to expand? How did our solar system arise? And that planet which, amid the powerful forces of the cosmos, is so temperate that life is able to exist on it (CCC 282–89)?

Genuine natural-scientific knowledge cannot be in contradiction with the faith (CCC 159). What no human science can explain, however, is that most fundamental question of thought: "Why is there something rather than nothing?" And further: How did it come about, in the process of the development of the universe, that precisely this planet appeared, and the life existing on it, and ultimately mankind? Whoever says that all this came about through the blind interplay of chance and necessity will have to explain how such an incomprehensible succession of "coincidences" could have occurred as were necessary, in the course of cosmic development, to enable the earth to arise as a life-environment for man. Specialists devoted to researching the preconditions necessary for all this speak of an "anthropocentric principle". Everything looks as if this whole development and its individual phases are governed by a master plan, of which we can discover, with amazement, only particular fragments. Faith tells us that this plan is the work of an infinite, wise, and loving intelligence (CCC 295).

The biblical account of "the work of the six days" (Gen 1) does not tell us *how*, in detail, heaven and earth came into being but does tell us *that* they were created by God and, further, that their great diversity was willed by the Creator ("each according to its kind"). The immeasurable variety of things in the world is an expression of the Creator's magnificence. We must therefore show respect for the individuality of every creature. That is the foundation for a moral approach to creation (CCC 339).

It is also implicit in the account of creation: among all creatures there exists a solidarity (CCC 344). All of them, large and small, have the same Creator, who has allocated the earth to them as their common life-environment. And all of them have a destiny that goes beyond heaven and earth, namely, the New Creation (CCC 1046), the eternal Kingdom of God.

17

Man

"What is man that thou art mindful of him?" To this wonder-filled question, the psalmist replies: "Thou hast made him little less than God, and dost crown him with glory and honor. Thou hast given him dominion over the works of thy hands; thou hast put all things under his feet, all sheep and oxen, and also the beasts of the field, the birds of the air, and the fish of the sea" (Ps 8:5–8).

Man—the crown of creation? Thirty years ago, Vatican II could still say: "Believers and unbelievers agree almost unanimously that all things on earth should be ordained to man as to their center and summit" (*Gaudium et spes*, no. 12). Today, many tend to see man rather as the destroyer of nature, the disturber of its peace. Is it not presumptuous of man to elevate himself in this way above the other creatures?

Years ago, Adolf Portmann, the great biologist from Basel, had already written: "The time is still not so remote when we were able to believe that the hues of the butterflies, the songs of the birds, and the splendors of the flowers had been created for our delight. This comforting deception, through which our existence was elevated so high as to seem the very apex of all life, is demolished by our first look beneath the eternally agitated surface of the sea." It is true: the world of the ocean depths does not concern itself with us, no more than does the overpowering expanse of the cosmos. And yet, only man can penetrate the depths of both the sea and outer space, uncovering—a little—their mysteries, and only he can realize that there is much he does not know.

Man's greatness does not lie in his strength—the lion is much stronger and the gazelle much faster—but in his intellectual and spiritual nature: he alone can know and love and therefore recognize that he knows and loves. That is why the Council says that man is "the only creature on earth that God has willed for its own sake" (*Gaudium et spes*, no. 24:3). And the *Catechism* explains: "He alone is called to share, by knowledge and love, in God's own life" (CCC 356).

Man's greatness is that he can become the friend of God. Anyone who sees man merely as a component of nature, as having no goal other than this earthly life, will find the psalm's statements about man's magnificence to be exaggerated. How different this appears if we allow ourselves to be informed by God's word that man has been created "in the image of God" (Gen 1:27). This unique status held by man we express through the term "person".

"Being in the image of God the human individual possesses the dignity of a person, who is not just something, but someone" (CCC 357). "Person", that is, not simply a number in nature's series, but an "I", willed, loved, and called by God. And whoever says "person" also says "community"—you, too, are not something but someone, an "I", loved by God just like me, and called to eternal life. Hence, "all men are truly brethren" (CCC 361).

18

Body and soul

That there is a difference between physical and mental realities is an experience familiar to everyone. A toothache is something other than mental anguish. Reflection is something other than digestion. And yet both sorts of thing pertain to the one person. We rightly say: "I" have a headache, or "I" enjoy listening to music. Man is, as the Council states, "a unity" of body and soul (CCC 364).

That man is a physical and mental being in whom the spiritual and material worlds are combined is a truth understandable to every one through his reason. Nonetheless, misconceptions about man that have serious implications repeatedly arise. For instance, materialism denies the existence of the soul and sees man as just a part of the material world. Conversely, the gnostic and esoteric currents that are so widespread today teach that man is, in essence, a divine spirit who has fallen into the alien, material world.

Faith comes to reason's aid here, confirming it in the correct view that man consists of both the spiritual and the material. The biblical account of creation expresses this in pictorial language: God formed man of dust from

the ground and breathed into his nostrils the breath of
life: "and man became a living being" (Gen 2:7). The
body and the breath of life are both God's work, but it
is the "soul" that first makes man to be man: through it,
he is similar to God, exists in his image (cf. Gen 1:27).

That is why the soul is also of more value than the
body (CCC 363). This was known to the martyrs
throughout the ages: it is more important to remain
faithful to God than to preserve one's bodily life at the
cost of betrayal. Thus, already in the Old Testament,
the aged Eleazar resisted attempts to force him to dis-
obey God's commands, saying: "I am enduring terrible
sufferings in my body under this beating, but in my soul
I am glad to suffer these things because I fear him
[God]" (2 Macc 6:30). Christ himself teaches us: "Do
not fear those who kill the body but cannot kill the
soul; rather fear him who can destroy both soul and
body in hell" (Mt 10:28).

This has nothing to do with "hostility toward the
body" (CCC 364). God could give no greater affirmation
of the body than through the Incarnation of his Son.
Christ was born in body, rose in body, in his glorified
body he sits "at the right hand of the Father", and we are
bound to him in body through the sacraments (cf. CCC
1116), especially through the Eucharist. We form one
Body with him, we are permitted to be members of his
Body (CCC 789). "Do you not know that your body is a
temple of the Holy Spirit within you . . . ?" (1 Cor 6:19).

Both body and soul are created for God. "The body
is not meant for immorality, but for the Lord" (1 Cor

6:13). Hence, we are obliged to show respect for the body, for our own and for that of our neighbor, and especially for that of the afflicted. "So glorify God in your body" (1 Cor 6:20).

19

Man and woman

The first word that man utters in the Bible is a joyous exclamation about the female companion whom God has provided so that he might not be alone: "This at last is bone of my bones and flesh of my flesh" (Gen 2:23). The first statement about man and woman is therefore that God created—that is, willed—man as male and female. That man exists in the differentially emphasized forms of maleness and femaleness is neither an accident nor a coincidence, nor, again, a blind whim of nature, but, rather, a splendid "idea" of God's (CCC 369).

Two truths are contained in this essential point: (1) that both man and woman share the same basic nature and are therefore equal in worth—both are fully equal as persons—and (2) that both, insofar as they are different, are in their own way "perfect" and likenesses of God. Being "male" and "female" is good; God himself has affirmed and willed this: "Male and female he created them" (Gen 1:27). In the Jewish prayer tradition, a man thanks God each morning that he was born a man, just as a woman does for being born a woman.

Man and woman have been created *for each other*. As the symbolic language of the Bible indicates, none of the animals is that "counterpart" to man that he lacks and without which he is lonely (Gen 2:20). We know how sad it is when a pet animal is expected to offset the loneliness of a human being (CCC 2418). Only woman, as his own equal, can be the "counterpart" of man. But the two are not, therefore, incomplete parts that would first have to supplement each other through mutual integration; they are independent persons who are meant to be "helpers" to one another. That they are attracted to each other is not explained in the Bible by assuming, as in the Greek myth, that each is part of a once-whole human being who, as a form of punishment, was "split in half" by the gods, with the result that both halves have been desperately seeking each other ever since. The love between man and woman has been conferred by God himself. In Sacred Scripture, its beauty, fire, indestructible force (cf. Song 8:6), devotion, and fruitfulness are the preferred images through which God's passionate love for man is expressed (CCC 796).

Yet how does that constantly arising, and painfully experienced, disorder in the relations between man and woman come about? "Their union has always been threatened by discord, a spirit of domination, infidelity, jealousy, and conflicts that can escalate into hatred and separation" (CCC 1606). "According to faith the disorder ... does not stem from the *nature* of man and woman, nor from the nature of their relations, but from *sin*" (CCC 1607). A fundamental break in the relationship to God has also destroyed the original, divinely willed harmony between man and woman. Cooperative companionship was replaced by the will to dominate, and trusting interaction by mutual recrimination (cf. Gen 3:12, 16). Since then, man and woman find their way to each other only if their love has been freed of the effects of "original sin" through Christ's Cross.

20

Original sin

"I sought whence evil comes and there was no solution", said Saint Augustine (CCC 385). What is the source of the evil in and between us, between man and woman, between generations and peoples? Augustine did not find an answer to his question until he had found the one who has alone conquered evil: Christ. From then on, the certainty never left him that the name "Jesus" signifies "God saves". Jesus is the "God saves" of all men. If it is correct that Jesus has come, and died, for all men, then there is no man who would not be in need of Jesus: "Come to me, *all* . . ." (Mt 11:28).

All, including children: "Let the children come to me . . ." (Mk 10:14). They also have need of Jesus; he wants to be their "God saves", their "Savior", too. "Original sin" implies first of all that all men, without exception, have need of Jesus, the Redeemer. "The doctrine of original sin is, so to speak, the 'reverse side' of the Good News that Jesus is the Savior of all men" (CCC 389).

Original sin is a mystery of faith; we know about it solely through revelation. It cannot be grasped through reason alone, although one can demonstrate that this doctrine provides a reasonable answer to the riddle of evil. It is therefore important to know exactly what the teaching of the faith states about original sin, especially as false notions about this are quite widespread.

The faith tells us that, at the beginning of the history of the family of man, those who were effectively our first parents abused their freedom and raised themselves up against God (CCC 415). The language of biblical imagery portrays the consequences of that choice: Adam and Eve lose their original closeness to God and flee before him. Internal distraction and mutual recrimination, domination and appetite become definitive of the relations between man and woman; and death, previously threatened as a consequence, makes its entrance into human history (CCC 399–401). What is described in Genesis 3 we experience every day as the reality of the world.

But why the reference to "original" sin? Why is a child already stained by original sin as soon as it arrives in the world, so that baptism is conferred on it, too (CCC 1250)? Original sin does not refer to any personal guilt incurred by the descendants of Eve. It implies that all men (only Mary is excepted here) are lacking something: what our first parents have lost through their personal sin is—like an inheritance that an ancestor has squandered—lost both to them and to all of us, namely, the gift of man's original closeness to God and the harmony that arose from it (CCC 404). In a sense, we are all descendants of the prodigal son, and it is only after

God has presented us with the "best robe" of grace that we are again safe and at home (cf. Lk 15:11–32).

"Original sin" also implies, however, that, despite the grace of baptism, and with its help, we must struggle all our lives against the inclination to evil (CCC 407). It is something we inherit from our first parents. But if we struggle together with Christ, this is "the good fight" (2 Tim 4:7), which will lead to victory.

21

The devil

" . . . But deliver us from evil"—so the Lord teaches us to pray (CCC 2850). From what evil, however, should we be delivered? In the words of the Lord's Prayer, we ask: "Deliver us, Lord, we beseech you, from every evil . . . " (CCC 2854). This petition takes in all evils that can befall us, physical and spiritual. In her prayers, the Church cites examples of such evils: "From famine, pestilence, and war, O Lord, deliver us" (CCC 2327).

Despite there being much concern with these evils in the Lord's Prayer as well, the primary emphasis there is not on "evil things" but on "the evil one": "In this petition, evil is not an abstraction, but refers to a person, Satan, the Evil One, the angel who opposes God. The devil (*dia-bolos*) is the one who 'throws himself across' God's plan and his work of salvation accomplished in Christ" (CCC 2851).

Nowhere does it become more clearly apparent who the devil is than when he appears to Jesus. He is the tempter who, in the solitude of the wilderness, wants to bring about Jesus' fall precisely there where our first parents opened first their ears, then their hearts, and finally their deeds to his whisperings. "If you are the

Son of God . . . ." The tempter wants "to compromise" Jesus' "filial attitude toward God" (CCC 538). Yet he is utterly powerless in the face of Jesus' loving filial obedience. Jesus' exorcisms (expulsions of demons) demonstrate that the Kingdom of God has begun with him and that the kingdom of Satan has been conquered: "If it is by the Spirit of God that I cast out demons, then the kingdom of God has come upon you" (Mt 12:28; CCC 550).

Who, then, is this "strong man" whom Jesus, as the "stronger", has bound (Mk 3:27)? Scripture and tradition "see in this being a fallen angel, called 'Satan' or the 'devil'. The Church teaches that Satan was at first a good angel, made by God", who became evil by his own doing (CCC 391).

The Lord calls him "the father of lies" and "a murderer from the beginning" (Jn 8:44). To deny this reality, to turn the devil into just an anonymous "power of evil", is not only naïve but borders on blindness, when one considers the abysses of evil that have opened up before man in our century. "This dramatic situation of 'the whole world [which] is in the power of the evil one' (1 Jn 5:19) makes man's life a battle" (CCC 409).

"The power of Satan is, nonetheless, not infinite. He is only a creature, powerful from the fact that he is pure spirit, but still a creature. He cannot prevent the building up of God's reign. . . . His action may cause grave injuries—of a spiritual nature and, indirectly, even of a physical nature—to each man and to society. . . . It is a great mystery that providence should permit diabolical activity, but 'we know that in everything God works for good with those who love him' (Rom 8:28)" (CCC 395), for we believe: "The reason the Son of God appeared was to destroy the works of the devil" (1 Jn 3:8).

22

Jesus Christ

Jesus is "the heart" of our faith, "for there is no other name under heaven given among men by which we must be saved" than the name of JESUS (cf. Acts 4:12). These words of the Apostle Peter are included in the epigraph to the whole *Catechism*. Christ is the center of catechesis. The aim of catechesis is to put people "in communion . . . with Jesus Christ"—thus Pope John Paul II defines the meaning of catechesis (CCC 426).

If one asks what constitutes a Christian, the answer is first of all this: someone who believes that Jesus of Nazareth is the Christ, the Son of the living God. That belief is the rock on which the Church is built (CCC 424). To believe in Jesus Christ means quite simply: to love him with all one's heart, with all one's soul, and with all one's might. To love him as we can love only God (cf. Dt 6:4–5). For that is the special, unique thing about the Christian faith: that Jesus, a man who was born under the emperor Caesar Augustus and died on the Cross under the emperor Tiberius, is himself God, God's eternal Son, true God and true man. That is the incomprehensible mystery of our faith, "the gospel of Jesus Christ, the Son of God" (Mk 1:1).

Only in the light of this can we understand why believing in Christ also means following him and that following Christ comes before all other human commitments. How could a mere man ever say: "He who loves father or mother more than me is not worthy of me; and he who loves son or daughter more than me is not worthy of me" (Mt 10:37)? That can be demanded only by one who is himself God. How could a man ever dare to say: "Every one who acknowledges me before men, the Son of man also will acknowledge before the angels of God" (Lk 12:8)? Does this mean, then, that man's eternal salvation depends on his attitude to Jesus?

Is it possible, then, for anyone to be saved without Jesus, if only in him is salvation, if he alone is "the way, and the truth, and the life" (Jn 14:6)? How do things then stand regarding the many, many men who have never heard his name, who have had no possibility of learning to know and love him (CCC 846–47)? Jesus himself gave the answer to this question: at the hour of judgment, the Son of Man will reveal that all acts of genuine love of one's neighbor ("I was sick and you visited me . . .") were also directed at him: "As you did it to one of the least of these my brethren, you did it to me" (Mt 25; CCC 1038).

But then why continue proclaiming Christ so specifically? Paul identifies his reason for seeking with all his powers to win men for Christ: "For the love of Christ urges us on" (2 Cor 5:14; CCC 851). Whoever is seized by this love, whoever has experienced communion with Jesus' Passion and the power of his Resurrection, will feel the desire "to proclaim him, to 'evangelize', and to lead others to the 'yes' of faith in Jesus Christ" (CCC 429).

23

The Son of God

The title "Son of God" implies "the unique and eternal relationship of Jesus Christ to God his Father: he is the only Son of the Father; he is God himself. To be a Christian, one must believe that Jesus Christ is the Son of God" (CCC 454).

I will never forget that Moslem, standing in Karlsplatz in Vienna, who screamed out loudly—I was very close at the time—"Jesus is not the son of God!" I respect his deep conviction. For him, God is one, and therefore Jesus cannot be God. To us, however—by grace, through the faith—it is given to know and love Jesus as the Son of God. Paul catches the entire Good News in these words: "When the time had fully come, God sent forth his Son" (Gal 4:4). And when Paul tells the Galatians about his conversion, what he recounts is not the external events that took place on the road to Damascus but the relevant inner development: "When he who had set me apart before I was born, and had called me through his grace, was pleased to reveal his Son to me, in order that I might preach him among the Gentiles . . ." (Gal 1:15–16).

What had happened in the Apostle's heart? He had

no doubt heard of Jesus of Nazareth and had been convinced that this man was a false prophet, a blasphemer. That was why he had persecuted the followers of Jesus so passionately. But then it happened: God himself revealed to him that Jesus is his Son. Luke, the student of the Apostle, also reports: "And in the synagogues immediately he proclaimed Jesus, saying, 'He is the Son of God'" (Acts 9:20; cf. CCC 442).

Jesus himself had allowed his innermost secret to shine through when, in Jerusalem shortly before his Passion, he recited the parable of the wicked tenants to his opponents: The owner of the vineyard first sends servants to the tenants to bring back his share of the fruit. After they are all driven away and even killed, it is said of the owner: "He had still one other, a beloved son; finally he sent him to them, saying, 'They will respect my son'" (Mk 12:1–11). After God had, for hundreds of years, repeatedly sent his prophets (the servants), he sends as his final messenger his own Son! More than that he could not give, his love cannot manifest itself more greatly. Thus Saint Paul also says: "He who did not spare his own Son but gave him up for us all, will he not also give us all things with him?" (Rom 8:32).

But what is this "all things" that God wants to give us? Paul tells us: God has sent his Son "so that we might receive adoption as sons", and he has also sent us "the Spirit of his Son" (Gal 4:4–6). Being a Christian means believing in Christ, loving him, and following him. It means still more: "You are no longer a slave but a son", Paul says (Gal 4:7); with Jesus, in him, and through him, we are permitted to become, like him, "sons and daughters" of the Father (2 Cor 6:18).

24

Conceived by the power of the Holy Spirit

Every Sunday, we profess, in the Creed, that Jesus was conceived by the power of the Holy Spirit and was born of the Virgin Mary. That is the first article of faith about Jesus Christ. It is directly followed by the declarations about his suffering, crucifixion, burial, and Resurrection. It is, then, a profession that is obviously essential to the faith—otherwise, it could not be mentioned on the same plane as Jesus' crucifixion and Resurrection.

And yet hardly any other article of faith is called into doubt more extensively than this. Is not Jesus' virginal conception weakly documented in the New Testament, "only" by Matthew and Luke? And does it not look all too much like a "myth", a legend, an ancient Oriental tale about the gods? These and other similar objections can be heard in constantly new variations, not just today, but from earliest times. Even in the first century, Jews and pagans had mocked this belief of Christians (CCC 498).

There is probably only one sensible explanation for the fact that the Church has, from the first Creed onward, always professed faith in the virginal conception of Jesus: she knew about this through apostolic tradition, which can ultimately go back only to Mary herself. Only Mary knew the secret of her Son's conception. She was the first to have believed that "with God nothing will be impossible" (Luke 1:37). Then Saint Joseph followed by believing the angel's message that the child conceived in Mary "is of the Holy Spirit" (Mt 1:20).

Just as Mary and Joseph assented in faith to that incomprehensible and yet wholly real happening, so we, too, are invited to accept this mystery believingly and to receive it into our hearts. If we are ready to do that, it will also be unlocked to our believing reflection why God became man precisely in this way.

The *Catechism* says: "What the Catholic faith believes about Mary is based on what it believes about Christ, and what it teaches about Mary illumines in turn its faith in Christ" (CCC 487). If we say Yes with our whole hearts and our whole minds, in faith, to the great mystery of God's Incarnation, if we really believe of Jesus Christ that he is true God and true man, then it is not difficult to believe as well that he was born, as man, of Mary the virgin.

Christ was born "not . . . of the will of the flesh nor of the will of man, but of God" (Jn 1:13). His coming marks a new beginning in the midst of mankind, which is caught up in a history full of guilt and death. This new beginning could be inaugurated only by God himself. From his conception, Christ is "filled with the Holy Spirit" and is therefore defined in his whole nature and activity by the Spirit. He is the new man, the beginning of the new, redeemed mankind. Just as Mary conceived him in faith, so too, through the Holy Spirit, Christ should become formed also within us (CCC 503–7).

25

True God and true man

"Though he was in the form of God, [he] did not count equality with God a thing to be grasped, but emptied himself, taking the form of a servant, being born in the likeness of men"—thus we sing in what is perhaps the oldest of the Church's hymns to Christ (Phil 2:6–8). "In the form of God"—"in the likeness of men"! From its earliest origins, the Christian faith has always acknowledged both of these. The Church has had to struggle constantly to ensure that both were kept together. Again and again, the temptation arises either to deny that the Son of God truly became man or to dispute his divinity (CCC 465–68).

Preeminently significant here is the Council of Chalcedon in 451, which acknowledged that Jesus Christ is "truly God and truly man, ... one and the same ... in two natures without confusion, change, division, or separation". This mystery has a contemplative potential that is inexhaustible, especially if we contemplate the life of Jesus in its light. Everything that Jesus does and says and suffers is "divine-human". For he, "the Son of God ... worked with human hands; he thought with a human mind. He acted with a human will, and with a human heart he loved. Born of the Virgin Mary, he has truly been made one of us, like to us in all things except sin"—so the Council says (CCC 470).

How is this to be understood? How was, and is, God's Son a man? Did he know everything, could he do everything? Did he suffer like us? The Gospel tells us that, as a child, Jesus had "increased in wisdom and in years, and in favor with God and man" (Lk 2:52); and we may well assume that Christ had learned much that belongs to human life. On the other hand, however, we never see Jesus show the slightest hesitancy; when he speaks, his words are not tentative or groping but flow with unparalleled force: "No man ever spoke like this man!" (Jn 7:46). Jesus is familiar with the thoughts of men, "for he himself knew what was in man" (Jn 2:25). He recognizes what men think; he knows them before they meet with him (as in the case of Nathanael). Three times, he foretells his Passion and Resurrection to his disciples. Above all, however, he always knows, from his earliest years, of his oneness with the Father: "Did you not know that I must be in my Father's house?" (Lk 2:49).

Can Jesus do everything? If we believe the testimony of the Gospels, we must declare with the disciples: "Who then is this, that he commands even wind and water, and they obey him?" (Lk 8:25). Healings of all sorts, even of one who was born blind (Jn 9), the miracles of the multiplication of loaves, the raisings from the dead, but above all, Jesus' authority to forgive sins (Mk

2:7)—these are all proofs that Jesus does not act with mere human power but is "true God and true man".

His divine-humanness becomes nowhere clearer than in the mystery of his heart (CCC 478). It is with this heart that the Son of God "loved me and gave himself for me" (Gal 2:20).

26

The life of Jesus

During the course of the year, the Church celebrates the whole cycle of events in the life of Jesus, from his conception (March 25) through to his Ascension. These liturgical celebrations serve not only the purpose of commemoration. It is true that Jesus lived at a definite time, when Augustus was emperor of Rome. Jesus was crucified "under Pontius Pilate". All these things belong to the past, and we can remind ourselves of them just as we can of other events from an earlier time.

Yet the situation is different regarding the life of Jesus. For we believe and profess that Jesus is "true God and true man". Everything that he did and suffered as a man, between his birth in Bethlehem and his Resurrection in Jerusalem, was unique: not a transient human life, but the once-only life on earth of the eternal Son of the Father. Jesus' entire life is "divine-human".

The *Catechism* devotes a self-contained section to "the mysteries of Christ's life" (CCC 512–60). The word "mysteries" indicates that, "from the swaddling clothes of his birth to the vinegar of his Passion and the shroud of his Resurrection, everything in Jesus' life was a sign of his mystery" (CCC 515).

To inquire into Christ's life through the methods of historical science is surely justifiable. It is helpful to be aware of the history of those times, the conditions of life in Galilee, the religious customs and beliefs of first-century Judaism. Archaeological research has brought pieces of evidence about Jesus more clearly to light. Biblical scholarship has contributed much to construction of a historical picture of Jesus and his environment that is as exact as possible.

Every pilgrim to the Holy Land knows how touching it is to see the land in which Jesus lived. Yet what also moves us is the mystery of him who lived here. And when we reflect, in Nazareth, on the Annunciation, or see, in Capernaum, the synagogue where Jesus spoke his words on the "bread of life", or are reminded, at Tabgha, of Jesus' preaching from Peter's boat, then all of this is present. Nothing is simply past. It lives, because he who lived it at that time has risen, and lives eternally, in all his humanness, both with the Father and for us. "He remains ever 'in the presence of God on our behalf' (Heb 9:24), bringing before him all that he lived and suffered for us" (CCC 519).

Saint Ignatius of Loyola, in his little book of Spiritual Exercises, recommends that, when we meditate on the life of Jesus, we should concretely imagine the relevant places and scenes and also try to enter into Jesus' joy and sadness. This method is intended to have the effect that we not only regard Jesus as our model but seek to live together with him. For, as the *Catechism* says: "Christ enables us *to live in him* all that he himself lived, and *he lives it in us*" (CCC 521). The various liturgical celebrations, throughout the course of the year, of aspects of Jesus' life are aimed at enabling us to attain this full life-communion with Jesus Christ.

27

Jesus and his people Israel

One passage in the *Catechism* is this: "We believe and confess that Jesus of Nazareth, born a Jew of a daughter of Israel at Bethlehem at the time of King Herod the Great and the emperor Caesar Augustus, a carpenter by trade, who died crucified in Jerusalem under the procurator Pontius Pilate during the reign of the emperor Tiberius, is the eternal Son of God made man" (CCC 423).

Jesus is a Jew—Jesus is the Son of God: both assertions belong inseparably together. The *Catechism* puts unflagging emphasis on this connection. In our century, in which such horrendous crimes have been perpetrated on the Jewish people, it must be a matter of especially close concern for us to consider in detail the mystery of "God's first love" for his people Israel.

Our point of departure here must be the choosing of Israel. This begins with the calling of Abraham, through which all the nations of the earth are to be blessed (CCC 59). From Abraham's descendants, God formed his people Israel, to whom, on Mount Sinai, he disclosed his will and, with that, the right way to live (CCC 62–64). God's covenant with Israel "has never been revoked" (CCC 121). Jesus, his Son, came not to abolish but to fulfill it (CCC 577).

"The gifts and the call of God are irrevocable", Saint Paul says (Rom 11:29). But did Christ not contradict the Jewish law in many respects? Did the New Covenant not replace the Old? The *Catechism* attempts to give a clear, painstaking answer to all these questions (especially 571–98).

Christ was born "under the law" (Gal 4:4). He lived in obedience to the law of Moses and loved the temple (as the dwelling of his Father: CCC 583). Law-respecting Jews were, of course, offended by his authoritative way of interpreting the underlying meaning of the law (CCC 581). Yet nothing was a greater cause of offense than Jesus' claim to be able to forgive sins himself (CCC 587): "Who can forgive sins but God alone?" (Mk 2:7). Either Jesus is blaspheming as a man who made himself God's equal, or he is speaking the truth because, as the Son of God, he really has authority to forgive sins (CCC 589).

Jesus was certainly not rejected by all of his ethnic contemporaries (CCC 595). A faction among the Jewish authorities accused him of blasphemy, condemned him in a trial that had many unlawful aspects, and handed him over to the Romans for execution. However, the Jews are not collectively responsible for Jesus' death (CCC 597). What took place then in Jerusalem is much more the fulfillment of a divine resolution (CCC 599); behind Jesus' death lies not only the personal guilt of his opponents but the guilt of us all: "All sinners were the authors of Christ's Passion" (CCC 598). We have all crucified him through our sins. He died, however, for us—for those who sent him to the Cross at that time and for all of us who continue to sin today.

28

Christ died for us

"There is not, never has been, and never will be a single human being for whom Christ did not suffer" (CCC 605)—thus a Council of the early Church formulates this central element of our faith. Christ did not die by chance, his death was not a tragic accident, an unforeseen mishap. Jesus was delivered up to death "according to the definite plan and foreknowledge of God" (CCC 599). The deed of those who blindly handed Jesus over to death was permitted by God in his love in order that, through it, his redemptive plan might be accomplished (CCC 600).

We believe that the motivation for God's sending his Son into the world was this: "For us men and for our salvation he came down from heaven . . . and became man"—thus we pray in the Nicene Creed. Jesus did not come in order to live for himself. He became man "not to be served but to serve, and to give his life as a ransom for many" (Mk 10:45). It is as if Jesus' whole path was determined by this one great goal of his life: the redemption of man. His whole desire is for this "baptism" he has "to be baptized with" (Lk 12:50): the sacrifice of his life for the reconciliation of the world.

There is no other explanation for this desire of Jesus' than the Father's love, which he makes wholly his own: "In this is love, not that we loved God but that he loved us and sent his Son to be the expiation for our sins" (1 Jn 4:10).

Reconciliation, redemption, atonement, ransom—all these expressions in Sacred Scripture revolve around the one great mystery of faith: "Christ died for our sins in accordance with the scriptures" (1 Cor 15:3). On the evening before his death, Jesus disclosed this innermost secret of his heart to the small group of his disciples (CCC 610). In breaking bread, giving it to them, and saying, "This is my body which is given for you", in taking the cup, passing it to them, and saying, "This cup which is poured out for you is the new covenant in my blood" (Lk 22:19–20), he shows them why he is moving toward his freely willed death: he will bestow his life on them just as he now offers them the bread and the cup. But he does much more still: bread and cup have become his own flesh and blood, and what he performs through his death on the Cross also occurs at the Last Supper and, since then, at every celebration of the Eucharist, he bestows himself on us ourselves.

Jesus' death was a sacrifice. It was the perfect sacrifice (CCC 613). A sacrifice is perfect to the extent that it occurs out of love (CCC 2100). "Greater love has no man than this, that a man lay down his life for his friends" (Jn 15:13). Only love can really reconcile. Out of infinite love, Jesus atoned for the lovelessness of all our sins, that is, put them right again through his love (CCC 616). The Cross is the victory symbol of love.

29

He rose again

"If Christ has not been raised, then our preaching is in vain and your faith is in vain." What Paul wrote to the Corinthians continues to hold true today: "If for this life only we have hoped in Christ, we are of all men most to be pitied" (1 Cor 15:14, 19).

Our faith is without foundation if Christ died but did not rise again. If Christ remained in death, then his Cross was a senselessly cruel death that has redeemed us from nothing. Our love would be directed toward a dead man, a corpse, and our faith would be the remembrance of a man from the past, but not of him who has said: "I am with you always, to the close of the age" (Mt 28:20). We could place our hope in this life alone and would have to say: "Let us eat and drink, for tomorrow we die" (1 Cor 15:32).

"But in fact Christ *has* been raised from the dead, the first fruits of those who have fallen asleep" (1 Cor 15:20). The one "Paschal Mystery", the death and Resurrection of Jesus (CCC 638), is the central element of our faith. Just as Jesus' death really occurred, so, too, did his Resurrection. The Risen One appeared, it is true, only to those witnesses chosen by him, whereas everyone in Jerusalem was able to see him die on the Cross. Nevertheless, his Resurrection is an event that left behind certain historically verifiable traces.

The first such trace is the empty tomb (CCC 640). Not for even one day would Jesus' disciples in Jerusalem have been able to talk of his Resurrection if the fact of the empty tomb had not been publicly visible. Of course, the empty tomb is still not sufficient to prove that Jesus rose: his body could have been carried away (cf. Mt 28:15; Jn 20:13–15).

Only through Jesus' appearances to his disciples does it become clear why his body is no longer in the tomb: "He is not here, but has risen" (Lk 24:6). The witnesses to his appearances—despite all the differences in their reports—confirm that Jesus appeared to them bodily, visibly, and palpably, and that they could recognize who he was by the marks of his wounds (Jn 20:27). At the same time, they attest that Christ's body was not his revitalized earthly body (CCC 645–46). Through his appearances, we also gain a prevision of the nature that, at the resurrection of the dead, our glorified bodies will one day acquire (CCC 999).

Christ truly rose again! This certainty of faith is the foundation of our hope. It confirms that Jesus is really the Son of God (CCC 653), that his words are reliable and true, that he has the power to forgive sins, and that he died for us, indeed, for me. Because Christ has risen, he remains present in his Word, in the communion of the Church, in the poor and the afflicted, in his sacraments, in the priests, and "most *especially in the Eucharis-tic species*" (CCC 1373): "Christ [is] in you, the hope of glory" (Col 1:27).

30

He will come again . . .

Christ will come again. He himself has promised this, and it has been the hope of Christians from the very first: "This Jesus, who was taken up from you into heaven, will come in the same way as you saw him go into heaven" (Acts 1:11), the angels announced at his Ascension. "When the Son of Man comes in his glory, and all the angels with him . . ."—so the Lord begins his great discourse on the Day of Judgment (Mt 25:31–46).

"Come, Lord Jesus!": this cry of longing occurs at the close of the Revelation to John. It is a response to Jesus' promise: "Surely I am coming soon" (Rev 22:20). *"Marana tha!"* (Our Lord, come!)—thus Christians pray in the language of Jesus (1 Cor 16:22), especially in the celebration of the Eucharist (CCC 1403), when they proclaim the Lord's death and extol his Resurrection until he comes again. In the Lord's Prayer, too, we pray for this coming when we ask "Thy kingdom come" (CCC 2818), for Christ's coming is the coming of his Kingdom.

But when will the Lord come again? It is true that the first Christians had supposed that this "latest" or "last" day was quite close at hand (cf. 1 Th 4:15). But they never gave specific dates or deadlines. Jesus himself rebuked curiosity about such matters: "It is not for you to know times or seasons which the Father has fixed by his own authority" (Acts 1:7). "But of that day or that hour no one knows, not even the angels in heaven, nor the Son, but only the Father" (Mk 13:32). All speculations or would-be prophecies about the end of the world are therefore to be rejected in faith. Christ can come again at any time (CCC 673), but he has instructed us to remain watchful (Mt 25:13).

But are there not signs that we are already living in the last days? The *Catechism* says: "According to the Lord, the present time is the time of the Spirit and of witness, but also a time still marked by 'distress' and the trial of evil which does not spare the Church and ushers in the struggles of the last days. It is a time of waiting and watching" (CCC 672).

"Before Christ's second coming the Church must pass through a final trial that will shake the faith of many believers. The persecution that accompanies her pilgrimage on earth will unveil the 'mystery of iniquity'" (CCC 675). Sacred Scripture speaks of the "Antichrist" and his temptations, which blind many. Consequently, the power of evil often seems overwhelming and crushing. Our own century leaves us with this impression. And yet, with a view to the Easter victory of Christ, we profess: "Already the final age of the world is with us, and the renewal of the world is irrevocably under way" (CCC 670), for Christ has risen from the dead, he is the

"Lord of the cosmos and of history" (CCC 668). His Kingdom has already begun on earth, for his Church is, "on earth, the seed and the beginning of the kingdom" (CCC 669). Even now the Lord is coming. He is in our very midst.

31

I believe in the Holy Spirit

"To be in touch with Christ, we must first have been touched by the Holy Spirit. He comes to meet us and kindles faith in us" (CCC 683). The Holy Spirit is the soul of Christian life. Just as the soul of man is visible, not in itself, but only through its effects, so the Holy Spirit, too, remains hidden (CCC 687), although he is knowable by his "fruits" (CCC 1832).

Is the Holy Spirit not the great unknown, even among us? And yet he is so important that Jesus can say: "It is to your advantage that I go away, for if I do not go away, the Counsellor will not come to you; but if I go, I will send him to you" (Jn 16:7). And shortly before he returns to the Father, he says to the disciples, who are asking when he will restore the Kingdom: "You shall receive power when the Holy Spirit has come upon you; and you shall be my witnesses" (Acts 1:8).

We live in the time of the Holy Spirit. He is now that "other Counsellor", or "Comforter", who will stay with us forever (Jn 14:16). Through him, Christ is present in our midst; through him, we can call God "Abba", Father. The *Catechism* makes special reference to four effects of the Holy Spirit (cf. CCC 737; 1092).

He *prepares* men for Christ. Since the beginning of creation, he has moved, as the life-giving spirit, within all creatures; during the long history of the Old Covenant, he prepared the chosen people for the coming of the Messiah. He is the Spirit of Advent (CCC 702–16). Today as well, he opens the hearts of the faithful to Christ (CCC 1098).

He *manifests* Christ: "No one can say 'Jesus is Lord' except by the Holy Spirit" (1 Cor 12:3; CCC 683). The Holy Spirit allows us to recognize that Jesus is the Son of the living God. He reminds the Church of everything that Christ has said. "The Holy Spirit is the Church's living memory" (CCC 1099).

He *makes* Christ *present*. In the life of the Church, Jesus is not just remembered; the Risen One is himself present in his Word, in "the least of my brethren", and in the sacramentals. Wholly unique is Christ's presence in the Eucharistic elements, which are changed by the Holy Spirit into his Body and Blood (CCC 1107).

He *unites* us with Christ. Just as the Holy Spirit is the bond of love between the Father and the Son, so he binds together with Christ all those in whom he is active. He is like the sap of the vine that bears fruit on its branches (CCC 1108). Without the Holy Spirit, we are incapable of living as Christians. He is "the interior Master of life according to Christ, a gentle guest and friend who inspires, guides, corrects, and strengthens this life" (CCC 1697). He is also "the interior Master of Christian prayer" (CCC 2672). Thus we should earnestly pray each day: "Come, Holy Spirit!"

32

I believe . . . the Church

In the Latin text of the Creed, there is a subtle shift of meaning that is difficult to render in translation. The text reads: "*Credo in Deum*" (I believe in God); *et in Jesum Christum*" (and in Jesus Christ); "*Credo in Spiritum Sanctum*" (I believe in the Holy Spirit); but then, in contrast, for all the following articles of faith, no longer "I believe in . . .", but simply "I believe . . . the holy catholic Church" (*credo . . . sanctam Ecclesiam catholicam*), the communion of saints, the forgiveness of sins, the resurrection of the body, and the life everlasting.

The difference here is significant: we believe in God the Father, Jesus Christ, and the Holy Spirit, but we do not believe in the Church. Belief, in the strict sense of the word, is owed only to God: it is to him alone that we can give ourselves with our whole heart, our whole mind, and our whole will. We should believe no creature, not even the Church, in this manner (CCC 150–52). "Salvation comes from God alone; but because we receive the life of faith through the Church, she is our mother: 'We believe the Church as the mother of our new birth, and not *in* the Church as if she were the author of our salvation'" (CCC 169).

That, then, is the reason why, in the Creed, we profess one holy Church but do not say that we believe *in* the Church: "so as not to confuse God with his works and to attribute clearly to God's goodness *all* the gifts he has bestowed on his Church" (CCC 750).

The first statement by the Second Vatican Council on the Church—the solemn prelude to all the subsequent expositions on her mystery and her life—points in the same direction: "Christ is the light of humanity; and it is, accordingly, the heart-felt desire of this sacred Council, being gathered together in the Holy Spirit, that, by proclaiming his Gospel to every creature, it may bring to all men that light of Christ which shines out visibly from the Church." The *Catechism* explains: "The Church has no other light than Christ's"; she is like the moon, all of whose light comes from the sun (CCC 748).

We cannot reflect on this enough: the Church is wholly dependent on her fundamental source, the triune God. It is from him that her life flows forth. If she were merely a human institution, she would not have withstood all the storms and had the power to renew and rejuvenate herself continually (CCC 175). The most important of the names and images used to characterize her all allude to this dependence, which does not signify lack of freedom for the Church but the most essential mystery of her life: she is the people of God, the Body of Christ, and is called his bride and the temple of the Holy Spirit (CCC 753–57). The more we understand the Church in this way, the more we will realize something that was the heartfelt desire not only of the Council but also of Christ himself: that, through the Church, the light of his gospel might shine forth to all men.

33

How did the Church begin?

Vatican II answers this question by first giving, not a historical account of the beginnings of the Church in Jerusalem and Galilee, but, rather, a powerful vision of the whole of human history and its origin in God's heart, in a resolution of his love (CCC 758).

The "idea" of the Church is as old as God's plan for creating the world (CCC 760). The world is not a product of chance and blind necessity. It was created and willed by God. Its goal is the "family of God", in which all creatures become united with their Creator. Since sin destroyed this communion and brought discord, hatred, and death into the world, God has started to regather his family (CCC 761): with one individual, Abraham, and with one people, Israel. Through these chosen ones, all peoples are to be blessed and gathered together (CCC 762). Thus the Old Covenant is already the prehistory of the Church.

It is often asked: Did Jesus ever really want to found a Church? He had, after all, mainly proclaimed the Kingdom of God. The Council gives a clear answer to this: "The Lord Jesus inaugurated his Church by preaching the Good News, that is, the coming of the

Reign of God, promised over the ages in the scriptures" (CCC 763). The Kingdom of God begins with Christ himself; in his words and deeds, in his Person, it is present. From the very beginning, however, Jesus had gathered men around him, in order to form his family. To this "little flock" God entrusted the Kingdom (Lk 12:32). That is why the Council says that the Church is, on earth, "the seed and the beginning of that kingdom" (CCC 768).

Christ also, however, gave his communion an ordered structure: the way of living set out in the Sermon on the Mount, its own prayer (the Lord's Prayer), and a leadership of the Twelve, who are also called apostles. Thus it is correct to say that Jesus willed his Church and founded her himself (CCC 765). This Church is not a mere idea; she lives on in history under the leadership of the successors of Saint Peter and the other apostles (CCC 816).

The mystery of the Church's life, however, is that her founder was not some long-deceased, great "religious founder" but the risen, present Lord: "And lo, I am with you always, to the close of the age" (Mt 28:20). Christ lives in the Church through his Holy Spirit (CCC 767). The latter is the "giver of life", in a sense, "the soul of the Church" (CCC 797). All the vital activities of the Church stem from him.

Hence, the Church is as broad as the history of man: foreseen in God's plan for creation, prepared under the Old Covenant, founded by Christ, animated by the Holy Spirit, "the Church progresses on her pilgrimage amidst this world's persecutions and God's consolations" (CCC 769). She will attain perfection only when all the elect are one day gathered together in the family of God.

34

The people of God

The Church is the "visible plan of God's love for humanity", Pope Paul VI once said (CCC 776). For Vatican II, the Church is as wide and large as God's own resolution; she is its realization in the history of humanity. For this, the Council uses the term "people of God". That term is expressive, to many, of the "spirit of the Council". Thus it is important to attend precisely to just what the Council means by it. For the notion of "people" has a quite special sense here, clearly distinguished from all earthly people, races, or political or religious groups.

"God . . . has willed to make men holy and save them, not as individuals without any bond or link between them, but rather to make them into a people who might acknowledge him and serve him in holiness" (CCC 781). In order to understand the special nature of the people of God, we must think of the original unity of the human race (CCC 360). In the biblical view, all men are bound together through their common origin in God, all have the same human nature and the same human dignity (CCC 1934), all have been entrusted with the same earth as their common life-environment (CCC 2402), all have been set a common goal by God, namely, eternal beatific communion with him (CCC 1718).

Under a merely individualistic view of man, such as is often advocated and practiced today, it is difficult to understand the Church as the people of God. Our feeling for the nature of the Church also depends on whether we have a sense for the "communal character of the human vocation" (CCC 1878). Perhaps many turn away from the Church today partly because, as Pope Pius XII already said in 1939, "the law of solidarity and charity" is so widely disregarded (CCC 1939).

The Council sees the Church as being "like a sacrament—a sign and instrument, that is, of communion with God and of unity among all men" (CCC 775). Precisely that is also meant by the term "people of God".

All peoples belong to God, and God is not the "private property" of any particular people; but he has acquired "his own people" from among all linguistic groups, races, peoples, and nations. No one belongs to this solely by virtue of birth. Baptism makes one a member of the people of God. Thus, in the strict sense, there are no "Christian peoples" and also no "Christian Europe", since the faith through which someone becomes a member of the people of God must be re-accepted personally and lived anew in each generation.

The people of God also have no earthly homeland but are on pilgrimage to the heavenly one (CCC 769). If we understand ourselves as the pilgrim people of God

(CCC 1045), then we will be happy to accept the privations of being wayfarers, then we will feel moved to share with those who suffer want here. In them we encounter Christ, the head of the people of God. It is both with him and toward him that we are on the way.

35

The Church—the Body of Christ

In the Letter to the Hebrews (10:5–7), the following is said about the Christmas mystery of the Incarnation: "Consequently, when Christ came into the world, he said, 'Sacrifices and offerings you have not desired, but a body have you prepared for me; in burnt offerings and sin offerings you have taken no pleasure. Then I said, "Lo, I have come to do your will, O God"'" (CCC 462).

"Belief in the true Incarnation of the Son of God is the distinctive sign of Christian faith" (CCC 463). In the early centuries, doubts arose repeatedly about whether Christ had really taken on flesh, in a true body. The Gnostics held, for example, that it was only a phantom body, from which Christ had separated himself again before the crucifixion. Something similar is still taught today by Islam. It would be all too discomfiting: God as man, the Son of God in a true human body (CCC 465; 476).

Through his body, which he received from Mary, Jesus has become the brother of all men, for "by his Incarnation, he, the Son of God, has in a certain way united himself with each man" (so the Council states).

He desires that we, too, should become one with him, to the extent not only of being his brothers and sisters, but even more: of becoming one Body with him, members of his Body (CCC 521).

The Church arises out of this communion with Jesus: "Abide in me, and I in you. . . . I am the vine, you are the branches" (Jn 15:4–5; CCC 787). "The comparison of the Church with the body casts light on the intimate bond between Christ and his Church. Not only is she gathered *around him*; she is united *in him*, in his body" (CCC 789).

Becoming a member of the Church is more than just an external affiliation with the communion of the faithful. The Church is the people of God because she is the Body of Christ. Through baptism, we become united with the death and Resurrection of Christ; we become members of his Body and thereby members of his Church. Through the Eucharist, this communion with Christ is further intensified. We receive the Body of Christ and become what we receive: his Body (CCC 1396).

The one Body—the many members: that the Church is the Body of Christ also means that there is a multiplicity of gifts and tasks within the one Church but that no one of the members can exist for himself alone (CCC 791). If the Church is the Body of Christ, then she can do nothing without him. He alone is her head, and all the life of the Church stems from him (CCC 792), whereas the Holy Spirit is, in a sense, the soul, the vital breath, of the Body of Christ (CCC 797).

"Saul, Saul, why do you persecute me?" (Acts 9:4): whoever persecutes the Church persecutes Christ, so intimate is the unity between the Church's head and members. He suffers in his suffering members, and we are permitted to be joined to him through our suffering. Thus his Body, the Church, grows toward him, until all the members are perfected with him (CCC 794).

36

The Church is one

In the Creed, we profess that the Church is "one, holy, catholic, and apostolic". These characteristics of the Church are so essential that they need to be considered separately here. It should be kept in mind from the start that the properties of the Church can ultimately be grasped only in faith, even if much in the history and life of the Church makes manifest that she is really one and holy, catholic, and apostolic (CCC 812).

Does the Church show herself to be "one"? Everywhere we run up against disunity among Christians. The many Christian confessions, the disagreements among Catholics—these seem to contradict the first essential attribute of the Church. Here, it is necessary to see, in the light of faith, just what sort of "oneness" is meant.

The *Catechism* considers the unity of the Church from the standpoint of her origin. Christ's instruction to make all men his disciples means that God wants to gather the one family of man, driven apart as the result of sin, into the communion of his people. The Church is the beginning of the one family of God (CCC 761). She will be perfected in God's Kingdom (CCC 769).

All men are called to this unity, with all the differences among their cultures and their gifts. Their living diversity is no obstacle to unity but makes up the richness of the Church (CCC 1201). Nonetheless, unity is constantly threatened and is attainable only with difficulty.

We must not forget that original sin, with its attendant inclination to evil, has introduced a constantly active "bacterium" into the world (CCC 400–401; 407–8). Every sin, including the most hidden one, subverts or destroys unity. That is why, from the very beginning, there have been lesser and greater divisions within the Church (CCC 817). The first, and deepest, rift is the split within the people of Israel, only one part of which acknowledged Jesus as its Messiah. Thus we are full of longing in our appeals that the people which was first chosen by God's love might fully acknowledge Jesus Christ (CCC 674).

Down through the centuries, numerous other rifts have occurred within the communion of the Church, imposing a heavy burden on the witness of Christians and often being a hindrance to the spread of the faith (CCC 855). The Holy Spirit therefore urges Christians to seek the pathway to unity. That can only be Christ himself. He "reconciled all men to God by the cross, . . . restoring the unity of all in one people and one body" (CCC 813).

But does, then, the "one" Church exist? Some think that this will not come about until the end. Yet the Council teaches that the one Church of Jesus Christ "subsists in the Catholic Church" (CCC 816). Christ has founded *one* Church. She is alive there where Peter and his successors are. Yet many elements of Christ's Church are also alive in the separate congregations. All these gifts of Christ's press inherently toward unity. Hence, the more closely we are gathered around Christ, the clearer the unity of the Church becomes.

37

The Church is holy

The second property that the Creed attributes to the Church is holiness. But how can the Church be holy? Does this mean that all who make up the Church are also holy? Is the Church a kind of person to whom one can attribute holiness? One thing is certain: God alone is the Holy One (CCC 208). We can draw closer to the holiness of the Church only if we have a feeling for the holiness of God. That requires having a respect for the immeasurable greatness of God and a sense for his protective nearness. In the presence of God, man becomes aware of his own smallness and wretchedness but also of the holy and healing dimensions of God (CCC 1502).

Whatever God touches becomes holy and healed. We call the Church holy because Christ "loved the church and gave himself up for her, that he might sanctify her, having cleansed her" (Eph 5:25–26). Just as all the Church's light emanates from Christ (CCC 748), so, too, does her holiness. Therefore we pray in the Prefatio I de Sanctis: "You are glorified in the assembly of your Holy Ones, for in crowning their merits you are crowning your own gifts" (CCC 2006).

When, in the Creed, we refer to the Church as holy, we are thereby acknowledging that she is "endowed with heavenly riches" (CCC 771). We see her, as it were, through the eyes of Christ, as his beloved bride (CCC 796). She is incomparably beautiful. Saint John envisaged her as the heavenly Jerusalem, prepared like a bride adorned for her husband (CCC 756). Were we only to see, in faith, how the splendor of Christ is reflected in the countenance of the Church, we would understand more profoundly why the Church is called holy.

Because Christ makes the Church holy, the Church can also make holy (CCC 824). Indeed that is the goal of all the Church's activity: increased holiness (CCC 2013). All the "means of healing" that are entrusted to the Church subserve that goal: the Word of God, the sacraments, the charisms, the offices and functions. Vatican II places this at the center of its expositions on the Church: that all are called to holiness (CCC 2013). The only measure of holiness, however, is love (CCC 826). It is the heart of the Church, and wherever there is love the Church's holiness becomes effective and visible.

This also provides the measure of how things stand regarding the matter of sin in the Church. One cannot say that the Church is sinful but, rather, that she includes "sinners in her midst". When the Council says that the Church is at once holy and always in need of purification, this is an appeal to all the faithful to follow "constantly the path of penance and renewal" (CCC 827).

That the Church can be called "holy" already here on earth is something for which we receive new evidence in each epoch through men who, in a special way, can be called "holy". In every period, it has been through those men who lived out the full measure of faith and love that the Church has been renewed. More than anything else, the Church has need of holy men and women today.

38

The Church is catholic

The Church "is catholic because Christ is present in her". That is how the *Catechism* (CCC 830) explains the meaning of the word "catholic", which means, in effect, "all-embracing". Because Christ is risen and reigns with the Father and the Holy Spirit, because he has promised that he will be with his disciples "always, to the close of the age" (Mt 28:20), the Church is always and everywhere catholic. Christ is the fullness, light, truth, and life. He alone is the wholly all-embracing. Because he is present in the Church, which is his Body, the Church is all-embracing, even when gathered in some one place as just a small group of believers (CCC 832).

That becomes especially clear in the Eucharist. For it contains "the whole spiritual good of the Church, namely, Christ himself" (CCC 1324). In it Christ himself becomes present, in body and blood, in his divinity and humanity, in the full love of his sacrifice on the Cross for all men of all ages (CCC 1374).

There is, however, a further reason why the Church is catholic. Christ has sent her to all men and all peoples: "Go therefore and make disciples of all nations"

(Mt 28:19). By virtue of this mandate from Christ, the Church is missionary in essence. Mission is a requirement of the Church's catholicity (CCC 849).

The notion of "mission" often meets with a lack of understanding today. Are not all religions pathways to God? Why should the Church be the "sole dispenser of blessedness"? Does the old affirmation still apply that "outside the Church there is no salvation"? If the Church is viewed in relation to Christ, then the question arises: Is Christ alone the way? Is there no salvation other than in him? Again and again, we are brought back to this original profession of the Church: "There is no other name under heaven given among men by which we must be saved" (Acts 4:12) than the name Jesus.

This is why we believe that all men are called to the Church, to communion with Christ (CCC 836). And why we believe that his Church "is the universal sacrament of salvation" (CCC 849). The Church Fathers made use of a concrete image here: the Church is like Noah's ark. Only in and through her can man be saved from the flood of the world (CCC 845). They understood this image primarily as a warning to those who are in the Church: If you jump overboard, thinking to save yourself without Christ's help in the Church, you will drown. Those, however, who, "through no fault of their own, do not know the Gospel of Christ or his Church, but who nevertheless seek God with a sincere heart, . . . may achieve eternal salvation" (CCC 847).

But why then continue with missionary work? Again, the reason is Christ. God "desires all men to be saved and to come to the knowledge of the truth" (1 Tim 2:4). Christ and his path are the saving truth. Paul is active as a missionary because he wants to win all men for Christ: "For the love of Christ impels us" (2 Cor 5:14).

39

The Church is apostolic

The Creed affirms—as the fourth property of the Church—that she is apostolic. That means literally: she has been sent. Sending is part of her essence. On Easter evening, the Lord says to his disciples: "As the Father has sent me, even so I send you" (Jn 20:21). Through his disciples, the risen Lord continues to be active until he comes again (CCC 669). Thus the "apostolate" (CCC 863) is as much a part of the Church's essence as is mission. According to the Decree on the Apostolate of Lay People by Vatican II, we call an "apostolate" every activity that is directed toward the goal of the Church: to spread the Kingdom of Christ over all the earth so that all men are enabled to share in redemption (CCC 863).

The first ones Jesus sent were his disciples, in particular the Twelve, who were therefore called, in a unique sense, apostles, or "those sent". The Church was, and remains, built "upon the foundation of the apostles" (Eph 2:20). She is the apostolic Church because she continues, even today, to build on the witness and teaching of the apostles (CCC 857). Initially, the apostles handed on what they had heard and experienced of Christ and what the Holy Spirit had taught them to understand. Thus Jesus' deeds and words have come down to us primarily through their preaching (CCC 126). Their lives are a mirror of Jesus, their beloved Master. They carried on what Jesus had committed to them, such as baptism and the celebration of the Eucharist. They also created institutions designed to further their mission (for example, that of the "elder", which they introduced into the congregations). Finally, they or their students, under the inspiration of the Holy Spirit, formulated what was to be transmitted in writing of Jesus' redemptive message (CCC 76; 106; 126).

The totality of what the apostles handed down, orally and in writing, we refer to as the "apostolic tradition" (CCC 75). Through it alone do we have access to Jesus' deeds and words. Hence, the apostolic tradition also remains the measure of the Church's faithfulness to her origins. All acts of renewal in the Church are also acts of retrospective reflection on the apostolic beginnings.

But the Church is apostolic in yet another sense: "In order that the full and living Gospel might always be preserved in the Church the apostles left bishops as their successors. They gave them 'their own position of teaching authority' " (CCC 77; 860). All that the apostles have proclaimed is to be perpetuated until Christ's Second Coming. Hence, "apostolic office" is among the essential constituents of the Church. The apostles' mission of being direct witnesses to Jesus and his Resurrection is, of course, nontransferable. In this, they remain a foundation of the Church. But Christ's commission that the apostles were to be shepherds of his people remains in effect for all time. The fact that the apostles, in their successors the bishops (CCC 861), continue to lead Christ's flock is another reason that the Church is apostolic.

40

The hierarchy of the Church

The Council and, following it, the *Catechism* have considered the Church first in her essence, the mystery of her life: her origin in divine resolution and her gradual realization within sacred history. The Church was presented as the people of God and the Body of Christ. Everything that was said there about the Church and her essential qualities (that she is one, holy, catholic, and apostolic) applies to all the members of the Church, is common to both priests and laymen: "In virtue of their rebirth in Christ there exists among all the Christian faithful a true equality with regard to dignity and . . . activity" (CCC 872).

And yet, in the one Church, there are different callings and tasks, stations and services. Only the most important of these need to be commented on briefly here. In particular, it is necessary to distinguish between the laity, those in religious life, and the hierarchy (CCC 873).

It is not enough to explain these differences as merely "functional": because every large organization has its functional divisions, so the Church must also have her hierarchical organs. Rather, all the services and callings within the Church need to be seen in terms of their relationship to Christ, the head of the Church. All the faithful have a share, through baptism (and confirmation), in Jesus' mission, in his priesthood. The whole of Christian life should be one of "priestly service" (CCC 1268; 1141), an extending of baptismal grace into every area of life. Nevertheless, Christ, in order to prepare his people for this, established distinct services and callings: the "hierarchical priesthood" (CCC 874; 1547).

Why, then, the ecclesial ministry? The *Catechism* identifies several reasons for this (CCC 875–79). The most decisive is: "No one can bestow grace on himself; it must be given and offered. This fact presupposes ministers of grace, authorized and empowered by Christ . . . to act *in persona Christi Capitis*" (CCC 875). Because this is a special mandate, it is conferred by its own particular sacrament: that of Holy Orders.

The Lord himself called and appointed the first of those who were to act with him and through him: the Twelve and, at their head, Peter. The Pope and the bishops form, on the model of the apostles and as their successors, a college that is headed by the Pope (CCC 880). The office of Bishop of Rome implies being "Vicar of Christ" and "pastor of the entire Church" (CCC 882). The individual bishops are, with the assistance of priests and deacons, the pastors of the "particular Churches" (above all of the dioceses; CCC 886; 1560). They exercise their pastoral office "personally in the name of Christ" (CCC 895), which is why the

Council can say: "In the person of the bishops, then, to whom the priests render assistance, the Lord Jesus Christ, supreme high priest, is present in the midst of the faithful" (*Lumen gentium*, 21).

The hierarchical priesthood is part of the Church. It is not her essence and also not her goal, but it is one of the means established by Christ himself to enable the Church to realize her goal: being the people of God and the Body of Christ (CCC 1547).

41

The laity in the Church

The *Catechism* devotes barely four pages to the topic of "the lay faithful" (CCC 897–913). Out of almost seven hundred pages of text, extremely little, one might well say. It would be a serious misunderstanding, however, to assume that only those few pages are concerned with the laity. Everything said in the *Catechism* about the faith and life of Christians applies to all the baptized. Hence, it is sufficient if, in a section on the "stations" in the Church, something is said about the laity as distinct from the hierarchy and those in the religious state (CCC 897).

The foundation here is the Council's doctrine of the threefold office of Christ: he was anointed by the Holy Spirit as priest, prophet, and king (CCC 783; 436). All the members of the people of God have a share in Christ's three offices, each according to his calling.

The Council stresses particularly the "worldly mission" of the laity: "so to illuminate and order all temporal things with which they are closely associated that these may always be effected and grow according to Christ" (CCC 898). This mission pertains to the Church as well as to the laity themselves: "They are the Church"

(Pius XII). Thus the Church exists wherever they are present (CCC 900): "Through them the Church is the animating principle of human society" (Pius XII).

In order to understand the priestly office of the laity, we must reflect on the common priesthood of the baptized. We exercise this, as the Council says, "by the reception of the sacraments, prayer and thanksgiving, the witness of a holy life, and self-denial and active charity" (*Lumen gentium*, no. 10). The whole of Christian life, from the most deeply realized liturgical experience to the simplest kind of everyday work, can be priestly service before God and to humanity (CCC 901). Our life itself then becomes a "blessing" (CCC 1078).

The people of God shares in Christ's prophetic office primarily through the supernatural "sense of faith" (CCC 785), in which the whole body of the faithful cannot err (CCC 92). For the laity, this feeling for the faith evidences itself especially in the testimony that they make through their lives but also through their direct public statements about Christ (CCC 905). "Evangelization" is a mission for all the faithful.

Christ exercises his kingship primarily by reigning in our lives: "For the Christian, 'to reign is to serve him' " (CCC 786). The people of God lives in accordance with its "royal dignity" when it recognizes, especially in the poor and the suffering, its thorn-crowned, crucified King and serves him (ibid.). In a wider sense, all social, political, and cultural engagement by the laity that is sustained by faith is a participation in Christ's "kingly office" (CCC 909).

"Intra-ecclesial" engagement by the laity in the areas of liturgy, teaching, and governance (CCC 903; 906; 910) is also part of their mission. This has expanded greatly since the Council. The life of the Church cannot be imagined without it. Hence, it is all the more important today that the laity should gain a new awareness of their mission to evangelize in all worldly sectors.

42

The life consecrated to God

"Teacher, what good deed must I do, to have eternal life?" To this question from a wealthy youth, Jesus responded initially: "Keep the commandments." When the young man persisted, Jesus gave a second answer: "If you would be perfect, go, sell what you possess and give to the poor, and you will have treasure in heaven; and come, follow me" (Mt 19:21). When the young Egyptian Antony heard this Gospel one Sunday in the third century, he was affected as strongly as if Jesus had been speaking to him. He went out, sold all his possessions, and took up a solitary life in the desert: the beginning of monasticism.

Like one great tree with many branches (CCC 917)—thus the life consecrated to God has grown since then, in constantly new formations; and even our age has seen, alongside the old monasteries, orders, and congregations, a profusion of new foundings. This station cannot be omitted from any conception of the Church; it "belongs undeniably to her life and holiness" (CCC 914), it is "a gift she has received from her Lord" (CCC 926).

To whom is Jesus' call directed? Only to certain individuals or to everyone? Is everyone called to a life in accordance with the "evangelical counsels" (obedience, poverty, chastity)? "Christ proposes [them] . . ., in their great variety, to every disciple" (CCC 915)—not to all in the same way, however, but only as "appropriate to the diversity of persons, times, opportunities, and strengths, as charity requires" (Saint Francis de Sales, CCC 1974). All are called to a life of complete love, but not all are called to the special station of "consecrated life" that "is constituted by the profession of the evangelical counsels" (CCC 914).

What characterizes this special calling? First, the proposal "to follow Christ more nearly, to give themselves to God who is loved above all" (CCC 916). This life is therefore to be defined wholly by prayer: "The consecrated life cannot be sustained or spread without prayer" (CCC 2687).

The principle of the imitation of Christ gives rise to a special kind of service to the Church. There are many forms of consecrated life: eremitic life and the state of consecrated virgin (both of which are experiencing a resurgence at present); monastic life with public vows and convent society; the secular institutes (the members remain "in the world", in their occupations, so as to exert a "leavening" influence)—common to all their members is the dedication of "themselves through their consecration [to God] to the service of the Church" (CCC 931). Even when they lead a totally secluded life, their calling is "missionary", it subserves the growth of the Kingdom of God. Saint Thérèse, who never left her Carmelite convent in Lisieux, is the heavenly patroness of the missions: "I realized that *this love alone* was the true motive force which enabled the other members of the Church to act; if it ceased to function, the Apostles would forget to preach the gospel" (CCC 826).

43

The communion of saints

The Church is communion through Christ, with him, and in him. Nothing can bind the faithful together more profoundly than this communion. It is what the Creed refers to when the "communion of saints" is professed.

The original sense of this word is unknown to many. It implies that the Church is a communion in the "holy gifts" (CCC 948). Among the members of the Church, there is a process of interchange, as with "communicating vessels": "If one member suffers, all suffer together; if one member is honored, all rejoice together" (1 Cor 12:26; CCC 953). This interchange occurs above all between Christ, the head, and those who are members of his Body. "Communion of saints" implies that Christ bestows his gifts upon the Church. What she receives from him is shared by all in common: his Word, his grace, his love.

Christ bestows his gifts especially in the sacraments (CCC 950). Hence, "communion of saints" implies that common bond which arises among the faithful through the sacraments, fundamentally through baptism and in a special way through the Eucharist (CCC 1331). The baptized are bound together through the new life they have received from Christ. Receipt of Christ's love deepens this communion. We become "one body" with Christ and therefore "blood relatives" with one another in Christ (CCC 1396).

Thus it is all the more painful when limits to the eucharistic communion become evident (CCC 1398–1401), as, for instance, when there are divisions in the Church or remarriages under civil law. These limits, if accepted in faith and with patience, do not entail exclusion from the "communion of saints". Even when the bond of communion is not possible, love can bind us together with Christ, especially that "preferential love" for the poor (CCC 2448). What we do to the least of his brethren, we do to him (Mt 25:40; CCC 678). No one is excluded from this "communion" with Christ, and ultimately it alone is decisive for our salvation (CCC 1038–39).

"Communion of saints" also signifies the relationship of those who are bound together with one another in Christ. This communion does not cease at the threshold of death. Those now departed who rest in Christ and those who are still pilgrims in faith on earth form a single communion: "All, indeed, who are of Christ and who have his Spirit form one Church and in Christ cleave together" (CCC 954). And just as there is an interchange of spiritual goods among the members of the Body of Christ who are alive on earth, so there is a similar interchange between the heavenly and the earthly sides of the Church. The saints who dwell in heaven help us. They are more closely united to Christ (CCC 956; 1370) and therefore also to us. When we love them, honor them, this strengthens our communion with Christ (CCC 957).

Finally, the "communion of saints" also includes those deceased who are still in need of purification. Our prayer is a help to them, and their intercession to us (CCC 958).

44

Mary—Mother of the Church

Mary is the summary image of the Church. Whoever wishes to draw nearer, in faith, to the mystery of the Church will look to Mary. The Council and, following it, the *Catechism* thus conclude their expositions on the Church with a chapter on the virginal Mother of God, Mary, in the mystery of Christ and in the mystery of the Church (963–75).

"What the Catholic faith believes about Mary is based on what it believes about Christ, and what it teaches about Mary illumines in turn its faith in Christ" (CCC 487). Who Mary is for the Church follows from her union with Christ. She is the Mother of Christ, the Redeemer. Hence, she is bound up with all those who are "members of the Body of Christ".

Mary is the "original model" of the Church (CCC 967) initially through her faith. In a certain sense, it was with her word of assent that the Church began. Mary is the first of all believers. Her unwavering faith is the basis upon which our faith rests. "It is for this faith that all generations have called Mary blessed" (CCC 148).

Mary is the "exemplary realization" of the Church because, following Christ, she "advanced in her pilgrimage of faith" all the way to the Cross. She suffered with her Son and joined herself with his sacrifice. She consented wholeheartedly as her Son gave up his life for us all. Beneath the Cross, she became the Mother of the Church when the dying Christ entrusted her to his favorite disciple, John: "Woman, behold, your son!" (Jn 19:27).

Mary is also the original model of the Church through having been taken up body and soul into her Son's heavenly glory. She is the first member of the Church to have already been fully perfected. In her, the Church has already reached the goal of her journey. Therefore, in a unique way, she also cooperates in the work of her risen Son. "For this reason she is a mother to us in the order of grace" (CCC 968). "She is mother wherever he is Savior and head of the Mystical Body" (CCC 973).

Mary is Mother, and the Church is also called Mother; and just as Mary is invoked as an advocate, helper, benefactress, and mediatrix (CCC 969), so those titles can be affirmed of the Church. In this respect, too, Mary is the original model of the Church. It would be a misunderstanding to believe that Mary's activity would take something away from Christ: "Mary's function as mother of men in no way obscures or diminishes this unique mediation of Christ, but rather shows its power" (CCC 970). Everything that Mary, as Mother, does for men comes from Christ and leads to him. The same also holds true of the motherhood of the Church, which is the "sacrament of salvation" for all men (CCC 776). There is, to be sure, a difference between Mary and the pilgrim Church: " 'But while in the most Blessed Virgin the Church has already reached that perfection whereby she exists without spot or wrinkle, the faithful still strive to conquer sin and increase in holiness. And so they turn their eyes to Mary'; in her, the Church is already the 'all-holy' " (CCC 829).

45

The forgiveness of sins

God alone can forgive sins. The scribes are right in affirming this (Mk 2:7). Because they regard Jesus as a mere man, they are offended by his saying to the paralytic: "My son, your sins are forgiven" (Mk 2:5). They have not comprehended that he, as the Son of God, as the Son of Man sent by the Father, "has authority on earth to forgive sins" (Mk 2:10; CCC 1441).

In order to appreciate the greatness of the gift of forgiving sins, we must try to grasp the gravity of sin. We spontaneously regard physical evils such as illness, catastrophes, or loss of possessions as the worst that can befall us. Yet moral evil, or sin, is "incommensurably more harmful" (CCC 311). Bodily and mental suffering can have a purifying effect and can reunite us with God (CCC 1501). If we accept it in faith, it becomes a participation in Christ's Cross and thereby a blessing for others (CCC 1521–22).

That can never be the case with sin. It separates men from God and from one another. It fractures the inner unity of the individual (CCC 400) and of society (CCC 817). What, then, is sin? "Against thee, thee only, have I sinned, and done that which is evil in thy sight"—thus the Church prays with the psalmist (Ps 51:4). "To try to understand what sin is, one must first recognize *the profound relation of man to God. . . .* Only in the knowledge of God's plan for man can we grasp that sin is an abuse of the freedom that God gives to created persons so that they are capable of loving him and loving one another" (CCC 386–87). Sin is "love of oneself even to contempt of God", Saint Augustine says (CCC 1850). Sin says: "I, I, I"—not thou.

It was for this that God sent his Son into the world, in this that the goal of Jesus' mission lies: "For he will save his people from their sins" (Mt 1:21; CCC 430). Christ "died for our sins" (CCC 601). Therefore the first gift of the Resurrected on Easter Day is: "Receive the Holy Spirit. If you forgive the sins of any, they are forgiven; if you retain the sins of any, they are retained" (Jn 20:22–23; CCC 976). What no man could ever himself confer was entrusted by Christ to his Church at Easter: the authority to forgive sins in his name.

"Baptism is the first and chief sacrament of the forgiveness of sins: it unites us to Christ, who died and rose, and gives us the Holy Spirit" (CCC 985). That is why our article of faith in the Nicene Creed acknowledges belief in: "one baptism for the forgiveness of sins" (CCC 977). But the power to forgive sins does not end with that. "There is no offense, however serious, that the Church cannot forgive" (CCC 982). Christ died for all men (CCC 605). In his Church, the door to forgiveness remains open to all who experience contrition.

46

The resurrection of the dead

"On no point does the Christian faith encounter more opposition than on the resurrection of the body" (Saint Augustine; CCC 996). Saint Paul had already been made to experience this when he began to speak of the resurrection of the dead. His educated hearers accorded him only mockery (cf. Acts 17:32). They believed in a continuance of life after death, in the immortality of the soul, in "metempsychosis". But why should the earthly body, the "flesh", be resurrected?

According to what we are told by public-opinion researchers (and caution is admittedly necessary here), 40 percent of us believe in "reincarnation", in "successive earthly lives", but not—as the Creed literally states—in the "resurrection of the body". How are we to account for (cf. 1 Pet 3:15) our hope in such resurrection? What grounds can we give that resurrection is "the confidence of Christians" (CCC 991)?

The first and decisive ground is: the Resurrection of Christ! Because he has risen again, we hope to be raised from the dead with him. For this hope we have two sorts of evidence: that provided by the "witnesses" to his Resurrection who "ate and drank with him after he rose from the dead" (Acts 10:41; CCC 995), and the everyday religious experience of all subsequent generations that the risen Lord is with us in his Word, the sacraments, the saints, and the poor, and that he dwells in our hearts through faith (cf. Eph 3:17).

The second ground is: the belief in creation (CCC 992). "For thou lovest all things that exist, and hast loathing for none of the things which thou hast made, for thou wouldst not have made anything if thou hadst hated it" (Wis 11:24). God upholds and sustains creation (CCC 301). To be sure, the material universe will pass away, as will our body, a part of it. Yet new heavens and a new earth are promised us (CCC 1042–50). In Christ all will be renewed. His risen body is already the beginning, an "initial deposit" on this new creation. Mary's bodily Assumption to his glory is the seal on the promise that we, too, will all be bodily raised (CCC 966).

Respect for the body (our own as well as that of another) follows from belief in resurrection (CCC 364). This body, which is a temple of the Holy Spirit and is nourished by the eucharistic Body of Christ, must be protected from abuse (CCC 2289; 2297) and kept holy. In believing expectation of resurrection, it is reverentially interred (CCC 1683).

Just how will we rise again (CCC 997–1004)? Here, our powers of imagination falter utterly. Sacred Scripture does not satisfy our curiosity but does teach us what is essential: it will be our own proper body, but not in its present form; an immortal "celestial" body, wholly accommodating of the Spirit, like the body of the risen Lord. But above all: it will be a life wholly with Christ. He is "the resurrection and the life", already now, and not just in view of what will be then.

47

Death

We are but strangers on earth who journey without rest, enduring many hardships, toward our eternal home. These words are from a Church hymn. The hope in a "resurrection of the dead" is the faith's answer to the "certain fate of death" that awaits us all. Death is both an evil and a good, an end and a beginning, a destruction of life and a gateway to life.

Death—an evil: "God did not make death, and he does not delight in the death of the living. For he created all things that they might exist" (Wis 1:13–14). To this statement from Sacred Scripture the objection could be made that death is simply a part of nature, since it has obviously been present ever since living creatures have been on earth. Is death not something natural and thus something willed by God? On the other hand, we often experience the death of a person near to us as something that ought not to be; and even the death of an animal can cause deep grief. "It is in regard to death that man's condition is most shrouded in doubt" (CCC 1006).

The world is not yet perfected. As long as creation is still developing, there will also be dying: "In God's plan this process of becoming involves the appearance of certain beings and the disappearance of others, . . . both constructive and destructive forces of nature" (CCC 310). Becoming and transience are intrinsic to a world that is continually changing. Not until God makes "everything new", when—in a way incomprehensible to us—he will perfect man and also the material cosmos, will death cease being part of nature (CCC 1044).

"Through the devil's envy death entered the world, and those who belong to his party experience it" (Wis 2:24). Death came into the world through sin, Saint Paul teaches (Rom 5:12). According to the Church's teaching, these statements in Sacred Scripture mean that "bodily death" is something "from which man would have been immune had he not sinned" (CCC 1008). Man is, to be sure, a mortal being insofar as his body is concerned, yet he was created by God "for incorruption" (Wis 2:23). Had man upheld his original bond of friendship with God, then death would have had no power over him. Still, God has, in his goodness, transformed death to a good.

Death: A Good—that is the title of a work by Saint Ambrose. During a period of great affliction, at the end of the fourth century, this Church Father wrote: "So when life is a burden, death brings release; when life is a torment, death becomes a curative." Death is a good, but only for him who has prepared himself accordingly in life.

Since Christ died for us on the Cross, "to die is gain" (Phil 1:21) for us, a departing to arrive "at home" (2 Cor

5:8), to be "with Christ" (Phil 1:23; CCC 1010). Whoever lives, even now, not for himself but with Christ can be separated by nothing from his love (Rom 8:38f.). Despite the terror of death, he will look forward to the hour of dying: onward to Christ! (CCC 1011–14).

48

Heaven

The concluding article in the profession of faith refers to the life everlasting. "Resurrection" and "the life everlasting" open the prospect of "the life of the world to come", of the "ultimate things" for man: judgment and final purification ("Purgatory"), heaven or hell as definitive happiness or unhappiness. Death is the gateway to eternal life.

When now, in the closing five sections of these "central elements of the faith", we reflect on the "ultimate things" in conjunction with the *Catechism*, something quite crucial must be considered at the outset. The Council states: "Already the final age of the world is with us" (CCC 670). Since the coming of Christ, since his Incarnation, death, and Resurrection, perfection has already come, the new life everlasting has already been conferred on us. In the liturgy of Easter Sunday, we are told: "If then you have been raised with Christ, seek the things that are above, where Christ is, seated at the right hand of God" (Col 3:1).

The life everlasting has already begun: "United with Christ by Baptism, believers already truly participate in the heavenly life of the risen Christ" (CCC 1003).

The passage from death to eternal life does not first occur only with bodily death. "For to me to live is Christ", Saint Paul says, and everything that binds us more closely to Christ signifies even now: life everlasting.

Still, the Apostle says: "My desire is to depart and be with Christ" (Phil 1:23). For as long as we are "away from the Lord", "we walk by faith, not by sight" (2 Cor 5:6–7). Only then will we first see God "as he is" (1 Jn 3:2), "face to face" (CCC 1023). That is the goal that every man, knowingly or unknowingly, longs to attain (CCC 30): "There we shall rest and see, we shall see and love, we shall love and praise. Behold what will be at the end without end. For what other end do we have, if not to reach the kingdom which has no end?" (Saint Augustine, CCC 1720; cf. 2550).

Heaven is perfect communion with the threefold God, with Mary, the angels, and the saints (CCC 1024). "To live in heaven is 'to be with Christ'." The glory of heaven exceeds anything we can imagine: "What no eye has seen, nor ear heard, . . . what God has prepared for those who love him" (1 Cor 2:9). We gain a "foretaste of heaven", however, if we simply take the path of love. Saint Thérèse of Lisieux praises this "heaven on earth" in her song "My Delight":

"I would like to live on for much longer, Lord, if that is your wish. Into heaven I would gladly follow you, if that is your pleasure. Love, this fire from the (heavenly) Fatherland, never ceases to consume me.

Death or life, what can they do to me? Jesus, my delight is in loving you!" Heaven is present wherever there is love; Christ has already brought it to us.

49

Final purification (Purgatory)

"Blessed are the pure in heart, for they shall see God" (Mt 5:8). We can receive the heavenly blessing of seeing God "face to face" (CCC 2548) only when our hearts are wholly purified.

Whoever draws near to God becomes aware of his own unworthiness. Before the burning bush, Moses veils his face. When Isaiah saw the glory of God in the temple, he exclaimed: "Woe is me! For I am lost; for I am a man of unclean lips" (Is 6:5). When Peter experienced the miraculous catch of fish, he fell down before Jesus: "Depart from me, for I am a sinful man, O Lord" (Lk 5:8; CCC 208).

Will something similar not occur after our death? In the presence of Christ and his incomprehensible love, will we not become conscious of our total unworthiness and wretchedness, about which we had been all too easily able to deceive ourselves in everyday life? The *Catechism* teaches: "All who die in God's grace and friendship, but still imperfectly purified, are indeed assured of their eternal salvation; but after death they undergo purification, so as to achieve the holiness necessary to enter the joy of heaven" (CCC 1030). This purification we call "Purgatory" (from *purgare*, to purify, purge).

The Church's teaching on Purgatory is very restrained. The Council of Trent simply affirms "that there is a Purgatory (place of purification)" but cautions against embellishments and speculations about the process of purification (CCC 1031).

How do we know that Purgatory exists? From the faith of the Church! How does the Church know this? From her practice, from her liturgical activity! An ancient maxim states: "The law of prayer is the law of faith" (*lex orandi, lex credendi*); "The Church believes as she prays" (CCC 1124). From her earliest beginnings, the Church has prayed for the deceased (CCC 958); she offers especially the eucharistic sacrifice "for *the faithful departed* who 'have died in Christ' " (CCC 1371; 1689), so that they "may find in your presence light, happiness, and peace" (Eucharistic Prayer I).

"The Church's faith precedes the faith of the believer who is invited to adhere to it" (CCC 1124; 166). From the practice of the Church we know that our prayers and sacrifices benefit the deceased (CCC 1032). This is also the purport of the indulgence that we can seek to win for the deceased (CCC 1472; 1479).

So many men are surprised by death and die unprepared. If today were to be the day of my death, would I be able to appear before Christ? How much is uncompleted, imperfect! How much have I left undone! Purification should begin not only after death. Already here on earth, trials, accepted in faith, are a "Purgatory". Severe illness can be a path to purification. The fire that ultimately prepares us for the joy of heaven is the love of Christ, which fills us with burning repentance and indescribable bliss.

50

Hell

In the great parable of the judgment of the nations, the Son of Man says to those on his left: "Depart from me, you cursed, into the eternal fire prepared for the devil and his angels; for I was hungry and you gave me no food . . ." (Mt 25:41f.; CCC 544). Jesus warns of the danger of being "thrown into hell" (Mt 5:29); he speaks of the "furnace of fire" (Mt 13:50), of the "outer darkness", where men will "weep and gnash their teeth" (Mt 22:13). "No amount of quibbling will help: the concept of eternal damnation . . . has its fixed place in both the teaching of Jesus and the writings of the apostles. To that extent, dogma is on firm ground when it speaks of the existence of hell and of the everlastingness of its punishments" (J. Ratzinger).

Just as clear, however, is the testimony of Sacred Scripture: God does not wish "that any should perish, but that all should reach repentance" (2 Pet 3:9); he desires "all men to be saved and to come to the knowledge of the truth" (1 Tim 2:4). God desires our salvation so much that he has "committed" everything to this: his own Son. He desires that we be saved, yet not without our own help. He created us without us. He does not wish to save us without us, Saint Augustine says. Because we have been created as free beings, it is appropriate to our dignity that God not force us to say Yes to his love.

Jesus complains of Jerusalem's obstinacy: "How often would I have gathered your children together . . ., and you would not!" (Lk 13:34). God's love waits for our assent until the very last moment. The criminal who turned to Jesus at the hour of death was saved: "Today you will be with me in Paradise" (Lk 23:43). But what if someone persists in saying No all the way to the end? "God predestines no one to go to hell; for this, a willful turning away from God (a mortal sin) is necessary, and persistence in it until the end" (CCC 1037).

The *Catechism* defines hell as a "state of definitive self-exclusion from communion with God and the blessed" (CCC 1033). The English writer C. S. Lewis says: "The gates of hell are locked on the inside" (*The Problem of Pain,* 127). He also formulated this striking aphorism: In heaven, man says to God, "Thy will be done"; in hell, God says this to man (*The Great Divorce,* 72).

Are there men who say No to God forever? While the Church affirms of particular men (the saints) that they are certainly in heaven, she declares of no one, by name, that he is certainly in hell. She does teach, however, that the fallen angels persist eternally in the hell of estrangement from God.

No one can make himself eternally happy. I can, however, make myself eternally unhappy. I can refuse the grace of conversion. Hell is a real possibility for each of us. Therefore the Church prays earnestly for all men: "Save us from final damnation, and count us among those you have chosen" (CCC 1037).

51

The Last Judgment

"For whoever would draw near to God must believe that he exists and that he rewards those who seek him" (Heb 11:6). Believing in God—this also implies assuming that what we do, or fail to do, has significance for him. Our acts have effects, perceptible and imperceptible, just as do our failures to act. Sometimes we are able to sense them immediately; often we do not notice them at all, and yet they are there. The priest and the Levite, who saw the robbery victim lying wounded on the roadside and continued on their way (Lk 10:30–37), possibly did not even notice that they had offended against the principle of charity. They pass by and forget. But their sin of omission remains in existence.

One day, in the presence of God, everything will be revealed: our deeds and our omissions, and all the limitless effects that followed from them and continued to exert their influence throughout the remainder of man's history.

Belief in a Last Judgment by God (CCC 1038–41) is an acknowledgment of man's freedom. Because God created us as free beings, we also bear responsibility for our actions and their consequences (CCC 1731; 1734).

When we are unfree through no fault of our own, nothing that we do can be imputed to us. It occurs involuntarily and will not be punished (CCC 1735).

Good actions deserve the recognition and gratitude of the community (CCC 2006). Much that is good, however, occurs in concealment and goes unnoticed by men. Who will reward that? Rewards and punishments by men cannot be the final word. They are often unjust. God alone knows of even the most hidden thoughts and deeds. One day they will be revealed and rewarded.

When? Christ says: "The Son of man is to come with his angels in the glory of his Father, and then he will repay every man for what he has done" (Mt 16:27). And Saint Paul: "We must all appear before the judgment seat of Christ, so that each one may receive good or evil, according to what he has done in the body" (2 Cor 5:10).

On the "Last Day", when Christ comes again, the "Last Judgment" will take place. In the presence of Christ, that will be revealed which is now often hidden beneath lies and appearances: who is really exalted in the Kingdom of Heaven. Then "the last [will be] first" (Mt 20:16).

For each individual, this "hour of truth" arrives already at the moment of his own death (CCC 1022): "At the evening of life, we shall be judged on our love" (Saint John of the Cross).

Even today, I can come to hear Christ's judgment of my actions: through the voice of conscience (CCC

1777). By recognizing myself as a sinner before him (for instance, in the sacrament of penance) and subjecting myself to his merciful judgment, I anticipate "in a certain way *the judgment*" that will come at the end of earthly life (CCC 1470). And when we begin, with rising alarm, to gain a sense of our unworthiness, when our own heart condemns us, then faith in the judgment of God's infinite love tells us: "God is greater than our hearts" (1 Jn 3:20).

52

Amen

The last word in the Creed is "Amen". With it, we also conclude this series on the "central elements of the faith". Two translations of this Hebrew word are possible: "So it is" and "So be it." Both are justified, both correspond to what those who recite the Creed acknowledge with their "Amen": "Yes, everything that we have just affirmed as the faith of the Church is truly and really so!"; and: "May it also be so within our own lives!"

"Amen" goes back to the same semantic root as the word "believe": being solid, trustworthy, faithful (CCC 1062). Thus the first and the last words of the Creed correspond to one another: "I believe"—"Amen." The "Amen" reinforces the trustworthiness of that which we believe. It is thus worth calling to mind again here a special quality of the faith, namely, its trustworthiness, indeed, its certainty. In the *Catechism*, we read: "Faith is *certain*. It is more certain than all human knowledge because it is founded on the very word of God who cannot lie" (CCC 157). This statement is surprising if considered only with a view to how weak our faith is. If, however, we consider it with a view to him whom we believe, then we find ourselves on solid ground. What we believe may seem obscure to us, something we cannot comprehend. And yet it is certain because God is trustworthy.

Sacred Scripture often cites two of God's qualities in a paired way: his kindliness and his faithfulness, or, as the New Testament says, his love and his truth (CCC 214). The word "faithfulness", "truth", has the same basic semantic root that underlies "believe" and "Amen". God alone is certain, only he can be relied upon. His words cannot deceive. "God is Truth itself" (CCC 215). Thus the prophet can speak of the "God of the Amen", that is, "the God of truth" (Is 65:16).

God's "Amen" is Jesus Christ himself (Rev 3:14). "All the promises of God find their Yes in him" (2 Cor 1:20). "He is the definitive 'Amen' of the Father's love for us" (CCC 1065). Hence, what our "Amen" at the end of the Creed expresses, first of all, is our praise, in wonderment and gratitude, of God's incomprehensible faithfulness and love, in which he gives us all things (cf. Rom 8:32).

When we close our prayer with "Amen" (CCC 2856), there are also overtones of the second meaning: "So be it!" This sense is central to the imploring "Amen" that occurs at the end of Sacred Scripture: "Amen. Come, Lord Jesus!" (Rev 22:20). Implicit in it is a plea that God might realize what he has promised, that what he has said and done might be consummated for us.

Our faith is endangered. We can make shipwreck of it (CCC 162). We must therefore pray for the gift of perseverance (CCC 2016; 2573). In order to remain faithful right to the end, we must beseech Christ, the faithful, to take our weak Yes up into his "Amen, Father" and to complete it (CCC 1065). Without his grace, we cannot attain the life everlasting that he has promised us, that he himself is. Glory to him, our whole love to him! "So it is"; "So be it." Amen!

Man's greatness lies in that
he can become a friend of God.

We are bound to Christ in the
Body through the ~~body~~ sacraments
especially in the Eucharist.

Holy Communion We form one
Body with Him, we are permitted
to be members of His Body.

The body is not meant for
immortality but for the Lord.

Mysteriously, however even our
evil actions do not fall out of
God's providence. In ways
that he alone knows he permits
evil and turns it into good.

(impulse - impulsive & separate from
insensitive.

God's patience.

Silence - to seek silence?

Jesus Mary and Joseph. I give
you my heart and my soul
true humility is to be found
in Jesus, Mary and Joseph.

They are the exemplary models
of humility.

They never hesitated or wavered
in their response to the will of God the
Father

To imitate Christ in his humility is truly something truly great.

Learn of me for I am meek and humble of heart.

Joseph remains silent throughout scripture - He never asks a question or gives a resp verbal response - He acts + his silence speaks volumes

"There are four virtues, the fruits of divine grace, which in their union bring the soul to God: humility, faith, purity and Charity. With the loss of the knowledge of the true God they were lost to the world and our Lord Jesus Christ brought them down anew from Heaven to Mankind. Their union in the soul is the distinctive sign of Christian holine